TABLE OF CONTENTS

INTRODUCTION	2
CHAPTER 1 | Population Trends	6
CHAPTER 2 | Urbanization	16
CHAPTER 3 | Disease and Globalization	22
CHAPTER 4 | Resource Management	28
CHAPTER 5 | Environmental Degradation	38
CHAPTER 6 | Economic Integration	48
CHAPTER 7 | Knowledge Dissemination	54
CHAPTER 8 | Information Technology	64
CHAPTER 9 | Robotics	72
CHAPTER 10 | Biotechnology	82
CHAPTER 11 | Nanotechnology	92
CHAPTER 12 | Conflict	100
CHAPTER 13 | Governance	108
CONCLUSION	116
APPENDIX: SOURCES	118
ACKNOWLEDGEMENTS	134
ABOUT THE AUTHORS	136
ABOUT THE CENTER FOR GLOBAL BUSINESS STUDIES	137

AN INTRODUCTION

Worldwide, CEOs and senior managers need to prepare their industries for Global Tectonics — the shaping forces and developing trends in technology, nature and society that will slowly revolutionize the future business environment. Much like earth's tectonic plates, global trends are quietly shifting the ground beneath our feet and transforming our industrial and societal topography.

History demonstrates that only a small number of U.S. companies that overshadow one wave of competition can continue to outperform the next. For example, consider that Sports Illustrated did not create ESPN; IBM hasn't been able to conquer its competitive markets like it did for mainframes; Digital Equipment Corporation used to outsell all minicomputer competitors, but now Apple and PC are household names; Blockbuster did not found Redbox or Netflix, and neither Macy's nor Sears has been able to outwit Walmart or Target. Many of these companies have experienced years of success in their market areas, so what could explain their fall? The answer can be found in the title of this book: Global Tectonics. Most business executives easily and often overlook such gradual developments — that is until a major seismic event shakes their corporate foundations. Yet, in order to remain on top, it's imperative that CEOs and senior managers anticipate the future.

Nearly a decade ago, we identified 12 global trends we believed would present the most formidable challenges to business leaders in the next 30 years. Though the same trends will continue to pose future threats to businesses, the context and data surrounding them have changed with the times. With the potential to further alter the arena, a new technological trend, robotics, has also emerged. Thus, we have decided publish an updated study of Global Tectonics with new statistics, data and information. Through reading this revised account, leaders will garner an understanding of what the global business environment will look like in the next 20 to 30 years.

Developments in areas such as demography, infectious disease, resource degradation, economic integration, technology, international conflict and governance will determine whether corporate strategies stay intact or unravel. These tectonic shifts will also determine whether industries have prepared for minor tremors or major earthquakes. When the dust settles, the tectonics will reveal the extent to which businesses have prepared for imminent change. Corporations have both the ability and the responsibility to foresee, to understand and to adjust to these trends as they unfold.

We categorize tectonic shifts as societal, technological and environmental. One set of global trends arises from the interactions of people with their environment. The global population is growing; cities are burgeoning, and these demographic changes impact resource management, health, and the quality of life for people and businesses around the world. Technology, another key tectonic driver, powers economic growth and development. Advances in biotechnology, nanotechnology, robotics and information systems have enhanced global economic integration, fueling the "knowledge economy." A third set of trends describes shifts within the international system and civil society. With advancements in technology and with the advent of multinational corporations and nongovernmental organizations, the way in which people interact has sparked a new way of global democratization. This has inherently led to changes in economic integration, governance and conflict that continue to transform the fundamentals of international business.

Many of these trends overlap in both degree and direction, which oftentimes serves to complicate the potential for industry to respond. For instance, the availability of land, labor and critical inputs, such as energy, depends on trends in population growth, biotechnology, urbanization and natural resource management. We also observe the growth of the knowledge economy and enhanced economic integration has risen mainly from developments in the field of information technology. Given the interconnectivity and synergy between such trends, business leaders must interpret tectonic shifts for their individual industries. While each tectonic has been analyzed on its own for this book, in order to truly be successful, executives must understand the relationship and interactions between the tectonics that pertain to their businesses. Every business, regardless of its size or industry, must view day-to-day operations in light of these global developments.

Our report is intended to facilitate this type of analysis by clearly outlining global trends and their potential impact on international business. The evolution of global tectonics will be pivotal in CEOs' decision-making process — both now and decades into the future.

POPULATION TRENDS

<-- *Guilin City, China*

Note: Chapter originally published in Industrial Management

CHAPTER ONE

By Fariborz Ghadar & Kathleen Loughran

Shifts in the nature and rate of global population growth are the first of the major tectonic forces we expect will shape the future business environment. Across the planet, demographic trends are transforming societies, modifying economic patterns, generating new economic and social dependencies, and altering geopolitical balances. How well businesses anticipate and adapt to these challenges will mean the difference between success and failure, opportunity and disappointment.

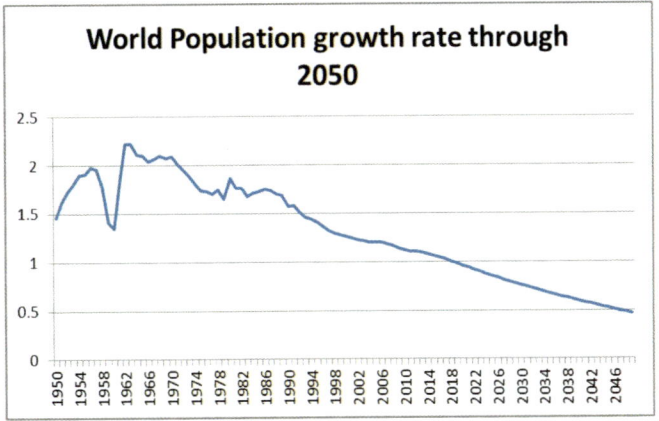

Source: United Nations Population Division, World Population Prospects, the 2010 and 2012 Revisions (Medium Variants)

What are the main characteristics of the population changes we can expect to see? The first and inescapable element is that the world population is rising quickly. As of August 2013, it hovered around 7.1 billion, but that number is expected to increase to some 8 billion by 2025 and to over 9.5 billion by 2050, according to the United Nations' 2012 world population prospects revisions.[1] Though this rise may seem to be incredibly significant, it is important to note that the overall rate of global population growth is not increasing at all. Rather, it is decreasing — and decreasing rapidly. This is the second key dimension of this tectonic force now at work. In the 1960s, when many analysts were concerned about the imminent "population explosion," the rate of growth across the world had already peaked. Since that time, the rate has dropped significantly by about 50 percent, from nearly 2.2 percent in 1962-63 to an estimated 1.093 percent in 2013 to a projected .853 percent in 2025, and to .468

percent in the year 2049.² In practical terms, then, many of us were worrying about a global population explosion at a time when the highest rate of growth in global population had already come and gone. The early projections of global population levels approaching 12 billion or even higher were simply way off the mark. Looking forward, accounting for these trend decreases in rates of growth, the absolute level of global population is likely to level off sometime in the mid-century, probably at just over 9.5 billion.³ Though the United Nations' 2012 revisions did show an increase in the projected 2050 population, it is still expected that after 2050, world population will begin to stabilize.⁴ In fact, in a 2004 long-range forecast of population growth to 2300, the United Nations concluded that, with the medium scenario, the world population would stay just under the nine-billion-person range. Another estimate, from the International Institute for Applied Systems Analysis, suggests that the aggregate population level will peak in 2070 at about nine billion persons and then begin a gradual decline.⁵

These latest projections are significantly different from many of the assumptions that have driven strategic planning decisions for decades. The revised projections suggest equally significant changes in the nature and growth of markets across the world. The fact is our population is growing most quickly in those areas of the world least capable of supporting such growth. According to a World Population Data Sheet released in 2012 by the Population Reference Bureau, 97 percent of the most recent surge in population growth can be accounted for in developing countries. Additionally, future population growth is expected to occur in the world's less developed countries.⁶ For example, at present both Spain and Tanzania hover around the same total population of 47 million; however, while Spain's population is projected to remain relatively the same, Tanzania's population is projected to grow to 138 million by 2050.⁷ On a whole, sub-Saharan Africa is expected to witness the "largest regional percentage increase in population by 2050," with a projected population of 2.3 billion by that time.⁸ Also, although Latin America and the Caribbean have lower projected growth rates, their combined population is still expected to increase from 599 million to 740 million by 2050.⁹ Asia, however, is forecasted to remain the most populous area in the world. Currently hosting more than half of the world's population, it will continue to grow, with an expected population increase of 1 billion by 2050.¹⁰ It is important to note that this growth will largely be determined by the individual growth of India and of China, for many of the more economically advanced Asian countries, such as Japan, South Korea and Singapore, are experiencing rates that have either slowed or have become nonexistent. While India is expected to continue to see rapid population growth, the same cannot be said for China. Most likely, China will get old before it gets rich because of government-issued controls on birth rate. According to an article written by Sergio B. Gautreaux for the International Policy Digest in 2011, nearly 13 percent of the population was over sixty years old, an increase of 10.4 percent from the decade prior.[11] These countries are emblematic of the overall trend that the most rapid population growth is occurring in those regions and countries least capable of supporting such growth.

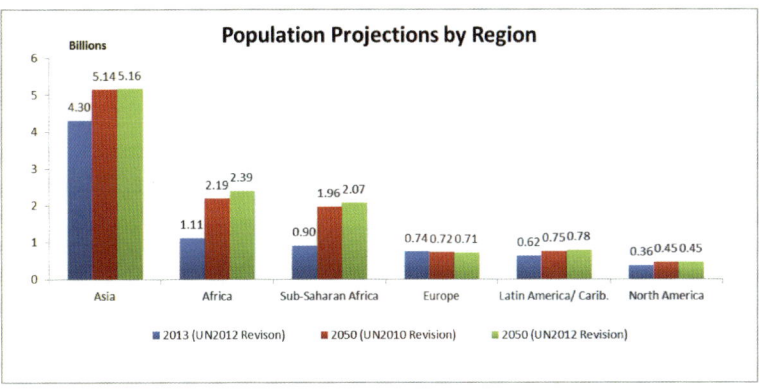

Source: United Nations Population Division, World Population Prospects, the 2010 and 2012 Revisions (Medium Variants)

The prospect of booming populations in areas of the world marked previously by geopolitical instability suggests additional complications in the future. In particular, the question arises of how well economies will be able to soak up ever-larger labor segments emerging from their "youth bulges." While the current working population is at an all-time high in both developed and developing countries, it is expected to fall in developed countries, declining from its current 608 million estimate to about 530 million in 2050 and 504 million in 2100.[12] Moreover, for the first time in history, it is projected the birth rate will be less than the death rate in developed regions by 2025.[13] The same cannot be said for developing countries, though; in these countries, the youth population is expected to reach 3.7 billion by 2050 and 4.1 billion by 2100.[14] Currently, the working population hovers around 2.6 billion in less developed regions. If these economies fail to develop opportunities, there will be increased chances of youth populations vulnerable to social, political, and religious radicalization.

Birth Rates & Population Growth

World & regional data	Total pop. in millions, 2013	Avg. annual rate of pop. change, percent 2010-2015	Total fertility rate, per woman, 2010-2015	Pop. aged 10-19, percent 2010
World	7,162	1.1	2.5	16.7
More developed regions	1,253	0.3	1.7	11.5
Less developed regions	5,909	1.3	2.6	17.9
Least developed regions	898	2.3	4.2	21.4
Arab States	350	1.0	3.3	20.6
Asia & the Pacific	3,785	1.9	2.2	17.6
Eastern Europe & Central Asia	330	0.1	1.8	12.9
Latin America & the Caribbean	612	1.1	2.2	18.7
Sub-Saharan Africa	888	2.6	5.1	23.0

Source: http://www.unfpa.org/webdav/site/global/shared/swp2013/EN-SWOP2013-final.pdf

These youth bulges can be expected to have a dual economic impact in Latin American, Sub-Saharan Africa, and Middle Eastern countries. In many of these states, large young populations will result in increased unemployment, resource scarcity, and enhanced demands for infrastructure, housing, education, and basic services. Increases in the relative size of the working population, though, will also attract labor-intensive industries and bolster economic growth. Many companies, such as Levi Strauss and Co. and General Electric, among others, have already moved to India, China, and South America where reduced labor costs bolster profitability. Some countries, such as India and China, have employed their vast pools of labor to reach higher levels of economic development. But as both India and China become increasingly developed, their wages rise, and so companies have already started to move to lower labor areas. Nonetheless, if these less developed countries, such as Egypt and other Middle Easter nations, are unable to provide jobs for their youth, they will continue to face political instability and unrest in the near future.

Countries with Highest & Lowest Fertility Rates

Highest	Fertility Rate
Niger	7.03
Mali	6.25
Somalia	6.17
Uganda	6.06
Burkina Faso	6.00
Burundi	5.99
Zambia	5.81
Afghanistan	5.54
South Sudan	5.54
Angola	5.49
Lowest	**Fertility Rate**
Singapore	0.79
Macau	0.93
Taiwan	1.11
Hong Kong	1.11
British Virgin Islandsl	1.24
South Korea	1.24
Bosnia and Herzegovina	1.25
Lithuania	1.28
Montserrat	1.28
Japan (No. 17)	1.39

Source: https://www.cia.gov/library/publications/the-world-factbook/rankorder/2127rank.html; 2013 est.

In contrast to the rapid growth we can anticipate in parts of the developing world, many developed countries will encounter stagnate population growth or even experience population contractions. In the former category of slower growth, we can put the United States, which by virtue of its immigration inflows can look to avoid some of the more pronounced pressures affecting other developed economies. In the latter category, countries like Japan, the Western European states, and the Eastern European New Independent States (NISs) of the former Soviet Union will encounter profoundly different situations. To varying degrees, each of these countries faces the prospect of depopulation, as they shrink at an anticipated aggregate rate of some 350,000 people per year. According to Population Reference Bureau's 2012 Fact Sheet, "Europe's population is projected to decrease from 740 million to 732 million by 2050."[15] For countries like Russia, their populations could be cut in half by the end of the century, thanks to low birth rates, decreases in life expectancy, and an aging population.[16] Japan is already experiencing challenges, such as economic stagnation, because of its low birth rate, which is currently at 1.39 children per woman (2.0 is needed for a population to remain stagnant).[17] Its population peaked and began to age a few years ago, and even more alarming, in the next 25 years, Japan's elderly population is expected to rise from one in four people to one in three.[18]

The upshot is that over the next 25 years, the developed countries as a group will drop in relative size, from an aggregate 20 percent of world population to around 15 percent.[19] A decline this significant clearly has serious implications for business and economic trends in countries around the world. In the Organization for Economic Cooperation and Development (OECD) countries, declining populations and aging populations will put a high premium on advancements in healthcare, medical facilities, retirement facilities, and insurance, along with a host of other geriatric-specific services. The burden of social security, health care benefits, and retirement costs will likely bring into question retirement age and the need to meet workforce demands.

The next and third key dimension of this tectonic force is the graying of humanity. Our population is growing old and growing old quickly. By 2050, it is expected that two billion people will be 60 years or older, representing nearly 25 percent of the world's population.[20] This would mean that the percentage would double what it was at the start of the century. In Japan, the proportion of elderly people relative to the working population is already the highest in the world. As stated previously, Japan's proportion of elderly people is expected to reach one in three people during the next 25 years. Italy faces a similar decline, in both the collapse of its labor force and loss of productivity. Even in the United States, the aging of which will be tempered by immigration inflows and by a higher birth rate, the population over the age of 65 already represents one in eight Americans. But, by 2030, it is projected that there will be twice as many elderly people in America than there were in 2009.[21]

On a whole, what will this mean to business? First, this trend will have a significant impact on the nature of economic activity, the rate of economic growth, the growth of markets, the demand for goods and services, the flows and volumes of capital, the availability of labor, consumer tastes and preferences, and the use of natural resources and "strategic" resources, including food, water and energy. Institutions across the board, from the largest governments to the most far-reaching corporations, will need to adapt to aging populations across the planet. How well prepared is your organization to adapt to aging labor pools, rising fiscal pressures from strained pension systems, rapidly changing consumer preferences aimed at ever older age segments, and new lifestyles geared to the old — to name just a few of the changes this tectonic force implies?

Secondly, the prospect for new inter-generational frictions in many societies, especially those with a rapidly diminishing worker-to-retiree ratio, is significant. How will governments confront the difficult choice between sustaining welfare and pensions systems that have been in place for decades and offering younger workers the same kind of lifestyles and social privileges that their parents have? Business could play a significant role in mediating these differences, by soaking up labor pools of older workers, by deploying new technologies that enable higher productivity at older ages, and by linking labor groups across countries.

Thirdly, these trends all suggest that demographic change will have a significant impact on the broader geopolitical balance. For example, will spending on old age crowd out the capacities of governments, especially in Japan and Europe, to maintain strong capabilities in national defense and foreign policy? For that matter, what role will problematic fiscal decisions have on stifling government investment in research and development? The geopolitical outcome will affect the risk premiums that corporations attach to doing business in less stable parts of the world. It also could have implications for more systemic scenarios in which instability cuts into global output growth.

Though children have long been regarded as the future of the world, in light of this global tectonic, we need to think in broader terms. Many countries can expect to see an influx of immigrants. Currently, legal and illegal immigrants already account for more than 15 percent of the population in more than 50 countries, and immigration from countries where population growth fuels unemployment will likely increase. Current trends indicate, however, that the absorption rate of immigrants into developed economies will be lower than the population growth rate in developing countries of origin. This scenario will most likely result in the implementation of stricter immigration laws, more border patrols, and an increase in the number of illegal aliens. LDCs will also have to work to keep their best-educated and most productive workers from relocating to other countries, a process referred to as "brain drain." Developed countries must weigh these negatives against the potential benefits of immigration, which can relieve problems created by a disproportionately large elderly population. While children still are the bulk of our future, the intermediate reality is that longer lives, declining fertility, shifting social patterns, and wider stratifications will all translate into a fundamentally different business environment across the planet.

URBANIZATION

CHAPTER TWO

By Fariborz Ghadar & Kathleen Loughran

In the decades ahead, urbanization (the migration from rural to urban areas) will become a predominant global trend. Today, over half of the world's population lives in an urban setting, and that percentage is only expected to grow. According to the 2011 Revision of World Urbanization Prospects, from 2011 to 2050, "the population living in urban areas is projected to gain 2.6 billion, passing from 3.6 billion in 2011 to 6.3 billion in 2050."[22] Thus, the urban areas of the world are expected to absorb all the population growth expected over the next four decades while the same time drawing in some of the rural population."[23] In total, by 2050, it is projected that 67 percent of the world will reside in an urban setting. Moreover, in the next decade or so, it is expected that populations in rural areas worldwide will begin to decrease.

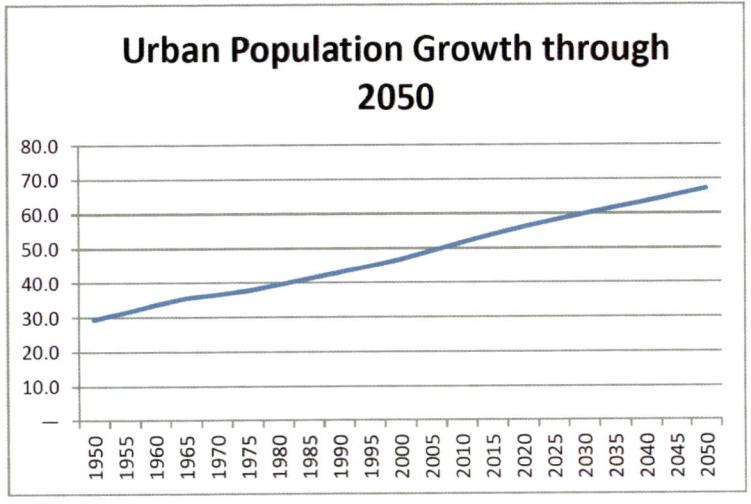

Source: United Nations, World Population Prospects: The 2009 Revision (medium scenario), 2009.

The Least Developed Countries (LDCs) will see the most rapid and extreme urbanization. As stated by the 2011 Revision, "Asia, in particular, is projected to see its urban population increase by 1.4 billion, Africa by 0.9 billion, and Latin America and the Caribbean by 0.2 billion."[24] Looking forward, urbanization trends that once dominated Europe and the United States will characterize Asia — a continent already home to 11 of the 15 largest cities in the world, including Shanghai, Tokyo, Beijing, Mumbai, Calcutta, Jakarta, Seoul, and Chennai. Each of these metropolises supports populations of 16 to 37 million inhabitants.[25] By 2020, more than 50 percent of the total Asian population will reside in cities, an increase of 35 percent from urban statistics in 2004. By 2050, China is expected to have the largest urban population of one billion, with India following shortly behind at a population of .9 billion.[26]

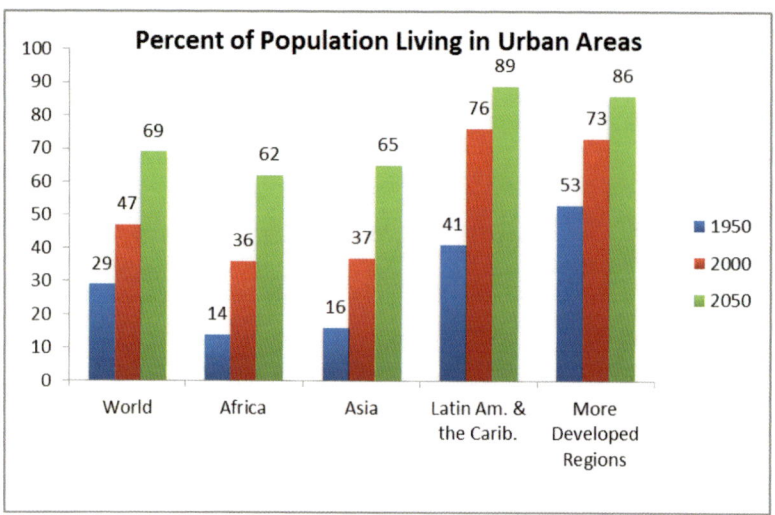

Source: United Nations, *World Population Prospects: The 2009 Revision (medium scenario)*, 2009.

China has already witnessed increased inflows of people into urban areas, causing issues not only for its people but also for its government. While people used to be restricted from moving to cities, reforms were implemented during the 1980s, which alleviated some policies on labor migration. As a result, numerous frequently uneducated youth migrated from rural areas into urban cities. Now, about 40 percent of the urban labor force is made up of migrant workers.[27] Despite their large presence, migrants still face many challenges, including the inability to register for a house, lower pay, and unfair working conditions. Moreover, the massive number of migrants has led to an influx of people that, when coupled with the global financial crisis, has resulted in numerous unemployed people living in cities. More explicitly, "In February 2009, Beijing announced that over one in seven — 20 million migrant workers — could not find work or had been laid off."[28] This, in turn, has the potential to lead to great social instability.

But China is not the only country wrestling with the issue of urbanization. In fact, compared to many countries, China is actually doing well. Mega-cities, metropolitan areas that support more than ten million inhabitants, will be a key byproduct of urbanization worldwide — and many will crop up in countries without the proper capabilities to host them. Though China has been able to afford managing these new population flows on a whole, other countries, such as India and many nations of Africa, will not be able to sustain these mega-cities. As a result, massive slums will emerge with the accompanying difficulties of poverty, health, and security. Presently, Asia already has 13 megacities to its name; however, by 2025, it is expected to have 22 of the world's total 37 megacities.[29] During this same time frame, Latin America will gain two, bringing its total to six; and Africa, Europe, and Northern America will each gain one, bringing each of their totals to three.[30] Tokyo, now the largest city in the world with a population of approximately 37.126 million inhabitants, will be rivaled in size by Mumbai and by Delhi, both of which are expected to reach over 25 million by 2025.[31] And Lagos has also recently experienced astonishing growth from 18 million in 2006 to over 20 million currently.[32]

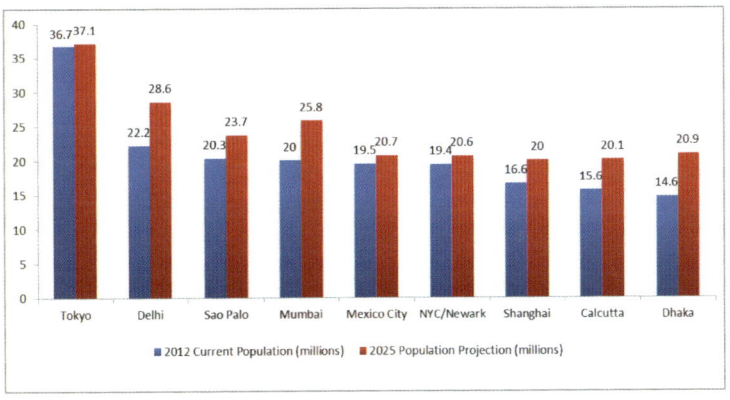

Source: United Nations, *World Population Prospects: The 2009 Revision (medium scenario)*, 2009.

The implications of this population shift — this tectonic shift — from rural to urban in countries across the world are profound. It will create tremendous new pressures on federal and local governments, which will be faced with the challenge of providing physical infrastructure and social services to ever expanding metropolitan populations. As China and other countries have already experienced, urbanization will also inherently lead to problems associated with unemployment, as businesses won't be able to sustain the massive swarm of people asking for jobs. Regardless, businesses will still be challenged to embrace the situation and to develop new opportunities to satisfy the increasing need for employment. Additionally, because many of these exploding metropolitan areas are situated in countries with little economic support and not enough available jobs, slums are bound to arise. The growing unemployed youth bulge will also lead to an increase in the presence of gangs. This will therefore present a concern for security and safety, which governments and companies will be forced to address. Even wealthy, developed countries, such as England, employ what could be considered drastic measures to ensure safety in their metropolitan areas. For a more explicit example, consider the fact that London has at least 500,000 security cameras installed throughout the city to monitor crime and to keep people safe.[33] Though these cameras have been marked by success, it is infeasible that LDCs could take similar measures. This compounding situation thus suggests the potential for unprecedented social, health-related, economic, and security volatility in the future.

Furthermore, rapid urbanization carries with it new challenges associated with rural development. Rural communities will languish as their populations diminish, and governments will likely attempt to develop their countryside to slow emigration to the cities. Projects providing rural areas with electricity, potable water, better roads, new transportation facilities, and employment incentives could improve living conditions and slow the demographic shift from country to city.

It's also worth noting that while most of the rest of the world becomes more urban, some predict the opposite will happen in the United States. According to Meredith Whitney, who wrote "Fate of the States: The New Geography of American Prosperity," much of America's business is relocating inland, taking advantage of cheaper taxes. Some businesses, such as Google and Amazon, have already begun the transition by investing millions to establish facilities in Texas. Even more evidential is that "In 2011, the flyover states contributed 25% of the U.S. GDP — that's up from 23% in 1999," which is financially significant.[34]

But what are the implications of urbanization for business specifically? The first area of opportunity will flow from the renewal and modernization requirements of mega-cities. The exigencies of size and population density in large urban centers will allow business to play an enhanced role in innovation, investment, and economic growth. Transportation shortcomings, improper allocation of resources, housing shortages, waste control, extensive air and water pollution, and city congestion will all take their toll on the quality of life in cities. As a result, businesses can expect to be presented with an opportunity to work with governments in rural development, which could ultimately serve to alleviate the burdens brought on by the rise of mega-cities.

DISEASE AND GLOBALIZATION

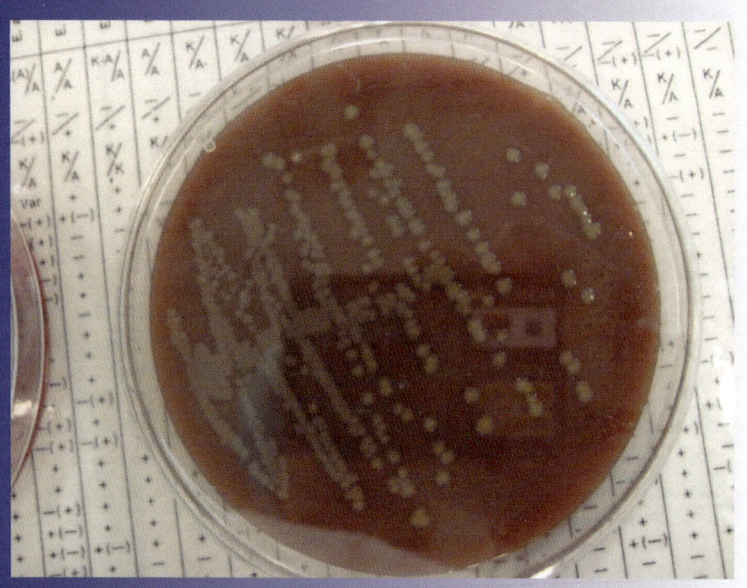

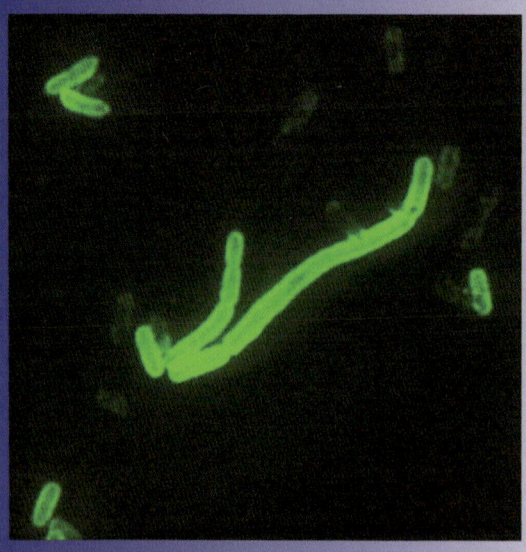

*Top: E. coli
Bottom: Plague, CDC/ Courtesy of Larry Stauffer, Oregon State Public Health Laboratory*

CHAPTER THREE

By Fariborz Ghadar & Kathleen Loughran

In this era of globalization, infectious disease thrives along with cross-border integration, including the movement of goods, labor, and transportation. While the spread of diseases and viruses used to be held in check by geography, the international community now already contends with viruses such as HIV, malaria, SARS, and tuberculosis. As people from different countries continue to interrelate frequently, more diseases and viruses are bound to spread quickly — and the stakes associated with this tectonic force are high. Infectious diseases kill millions of people every year and, as H1N1 or the swine flu demonstrated, they can quickly generate economic turmoil on a global scale.

Epidemics and the diseases that cause them are not new. Diseases have decimated the populations of every continent. In the 1300s, the bubonic plague, or Black Death as it was commonly known, swept through Europe, killing between 30 to 50 percent of the population.[35] Arriving in 1346, most likely due to new trade patterns and army movements, the plague moved quickly through Europe over the next four years.[36] The plague was a factor, at least in part, for altering the makeup of society. The massive loss of workers caused the demise of the feudal system, and the Renaissance was born. The story of epidemic and economic recovery is repeated over and over in the history of humanity. Business leaders must recognize the enormous impact disease can have on a stable world. The ruling class of the Middle Ages did not take into account the possibility of a disease drastically altering the fabric of their society. Today's business leaders can learn from that mistake. Europeans did not track the movement of the plague; they were unaware that trade was facilitating the development of the disease. Now, technology enables epidemiologists to study the movement of disease almost to the person. More is known about transmission modes, incubation periods, and the contagious nature of diseases. The World Health Organization and many governments have come together to monitor, track, and prevent epidemics before they reach the level of the Black Death. With new technology, however, comes a new challenge. We must contend with the speed at which people and goods move around the planet. Planes, boats, high-speed trains, trucks, cars, and every other type of transportation can move anything anywhere at breakneck speed. This means that diseases no longer take years to reach new geographic areas. Pathogens can arrive within hours. Travelers, business people, tourists, diplomats, and reporters become innocent transporters of deadly diseases.

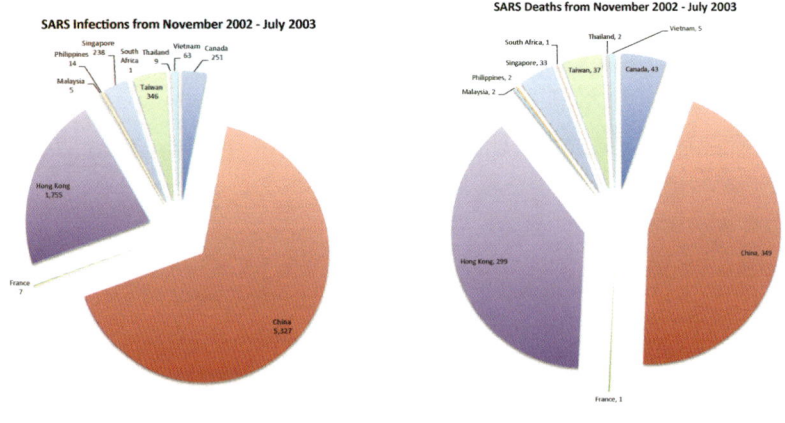

Notes: Total # of Infections=8,016; Total # of Deaths=774
Source: http://www.straitstimes.com/sites/straitstimes.com/files/ST_20130601_SAT6_3684266.pdf

As populations continue to interconnect, the likelihood of infectious disease epidemics and pandemics increases. The swine flu, for example, first struck fear in many United States' citizens, when it began to spread rapidly in the spring of 2009. By June of that year, nearly 75 countries were affected by the pandemic.[37] Because the Centers for Disease Control and Prevention was able to develop a vaccine for the virus, by November the illness' impact was minimized in the United States. Yet, the pandemic still had severe repercussions. The CDC estimated "between 8,870 and 18,300 H1N1 related deaths."[38] Because of a lack of confidence from the public, tourism, food, and transportation industries were hit hard, and the overall stock market declined. Fortunately, the H1N1 pandemic did not last multiple years; by August 2010, the World Health Organization had declared its end. Even though the pandemic did not result in a major recession, a 2008 report from the World Bank warns that a pandemic does have the ability to trigger a "major global recession."[39] Yet, the ability of infectious diseases to spread in a more integrated world is well documented. The 1997 outbreak of cholera in Peru, infecting nearly 10,000 people, occurred when a Japanese ship carrying export goods emptied its infected bilge waste into the Peruvian water system.[40] In other examples, Dengue Fever and West Nile viruses recently appeared in the United States. Also, African Prairie dogs, exported to the United States in 2003 as pets, caused a Monkey Pox outbreak in the Midwest.[41] Since trade and travel now link so many societies, H1N1-like epidemics and their human and economic consequences should no longer come as a surprise. Businesses must be able to adapt quickly to changed market conditions brought about by such epidemics.

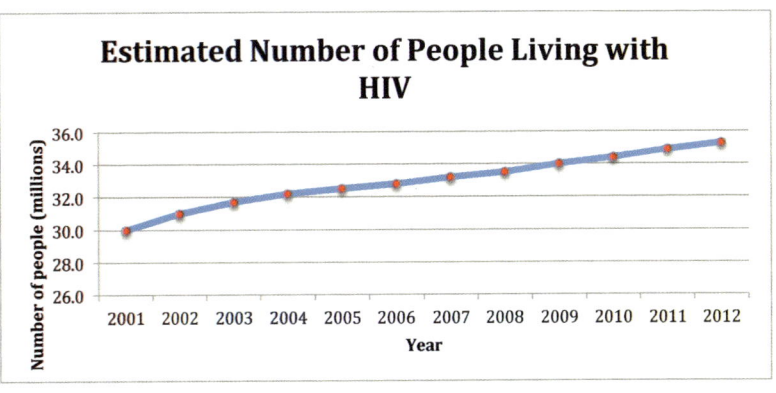

Source: http://www.unaids.org/en/resources/campaigns/globalreport2013/factsheet/

Unfortunately, many developing countries' businesses and governments do not have the financial means with which to do so. Infectious disease thus further impacts their economic growth and development, especially in countries with high disease burdens.[42] Moreover, those countries with the most underdeveloped public health services record the highest infection rates. Of the 33.4 million people now diagnosed with AIDS worldwide, for example, 97% live in low- and middle-income countries, with Sub-Saharan Africa reporting the majority of new cases.[43] In 2010 in Sub-Saharan Africa, an estimated 22.9 million people lived with AIDS.[44] However, according to the 2012 UNAIDS World AIDS Day Report, "Africa has cut AIDS-related deaths one third in the past six years."[45] Since the first reported cases in 1981, an additional 25 million people have died of AIDS worldwide.[46] Though treatment has improved drastically since this time, and eight million people are currently on HIV treatment, the infection rates will reduce productivity, GDP, and foreign direct investment.[47] Today, although there has been improvement in recent years, the AIDS epidemic still continues to rage in many developing countries that must also contend with malaria, yellow fever, and dengue fever. Together, these diseases have already orphaned millions of children, discouraged foreign investment, and impaired the education and healthcare infrastructure. The catastrophic social and economic effects will affect those countries for generations to come.

As we look into the future, the threat of biological terrorism must also be taken into account as a key potential force in shaping the business and overall environment. Following the terrorist attacks of September 11, 2001 and the subsequent release of anthrax in the United States postal system, many countries now work to prevent terrorist groups from gaining access to dangerous bio-agents. In 2008, the Commission on the Prevention of WMD Proliferation and Terrorism released a report that stated either a nuclear or biological terrorist attack was likely by 2013.[48] Although no such attack has occurred, it is clear that infectious disease has become an issue of national and international security for the entire global community. Smallpox is a case in point. Because many countries stopped their small pox vaccination programs in the 1970s, a biological attack with this potential terrorist weapon would create a humanitarian disaster.[49] In light of this threat, Israel and the United States recently vaccinated their military personnel.

So what does the natural spread of diseases and threat of a potentially planned one mean for governments and businesses worldwide? International disease control will present vast opportunities and challenges to businesses operating in afflicted countries or working to provide containment products and services. Ideally, countries need a global health infrastructure that responds quickly and effectively to epidemics, such as SARS and H1N1, or to terrorist-induced disease outbreaks. In this era of increased economic and social integration, an outbreak in one country can develop into a global pandemic in a matter of days. As a result, governments, non-government organizations (NGOs), and businesses must devise healthcare solutions that cross borders as effectively as the infectious agents they work to contain. Their combined ability to react and respond to outbreaks, and to devise solutions that meet the healthcare needs of the world's population, will be critical to continued global prosperity.

More specifically, what should businesses be doing to prepare for contingencies arising from natural or deliberate epidemics and disease-related volatility? First, they will probably engage in scenario-analysis in order to begin to define their reactions in the event of an epidemic. Second, they will most likely assess the extent to which international and national institutions are prepared for such contingencies, especially because public-private sector partnership is critical to defining and implementing solutions. Finally, the growing threat of bioterrorism suggests new possibilities for the private sector to marshal its resources and technological innovation in support of new biodefenses and procedures.

RESOURCE MANAGEMENT

CHAPTER FOUR

By Fariborz Ghadar & Kathleen Loughran

A key tectonic for the future is resource management, particularly the resources of water, food, and energy Over the next 25 years, businesses will play a key role in inventing and developing new technologies, such as desalinization plants, genomic plants, and renewable fuels, to help relieve resource scarcity. Corporations and governments will partner to improve food production and distribution, water system management, and energy efficiency in many countries currently facing shortages.

WATER

A critical resource monitored closely is fresh water. The reality is that only about .014 percent of the vast amount of water the Earth holds is available for human consumption.[50] Increases in the world population have led to decreases in available water. In fact, it has been reported that, "In 1989 there was some 9,000 cubic meters of freshwater per person available for human use. By 2000, this had dropped to 7,800 cubic meters and it is expected to plummet to 5,100 cubic meters per person by 2025, when the global population is projected to reach 8 billion."[51]

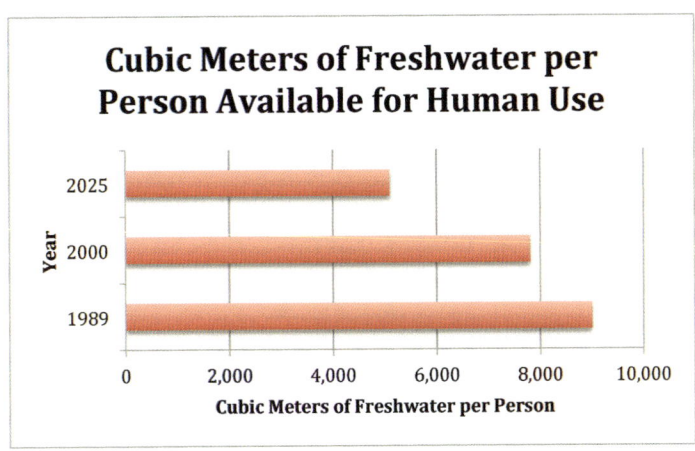

Source: Lenntech, a water treatment solutions company

Presently, one in nine people do not have access to clean water worldwide.[52] Because of this, in developing countries, nearly 80 percent of illnesses can be traced back to unsanitary water.[53] Moreover, this problem is only expected to escalate in the near future. According to UN Water Statistics, "water withdrawals are predicted to increase by 50 percent by 2025 in developing countries, and 18 percent in developed countries."[54] These shortages result from a natural lack of renewable freshwater sources and the large role of irrigation in agriculture. Additionally, climate change irregularities have increasingly become an issue related to water's availability. As stated by Cecilia Sharp, UNICEF's senior advisor on water and sanitation, "People cannot rely on rain water or groundwater recharge where they could before. You have a heavy drought and then flash floods where the soil is not prepared and you have soil erosion. How countries can adapt to these changes and understand them is crucial."[55] If current trends in population growth and water demand persist, these areas (specifically sub-Saharan Africa, the Middle East, and India) will face severe water shortages in the near future.

Not only does water's scarcity create issues related to health, but it also raises concerns about potential conflict between countries. Of the 260 river basins worldwide, 13 are shared by more than five countries, accounting for 40 percent of humanity. Although some studies have argued that historically countries sharing water resources have been more likely to work together than to fight, it would be remiss to think this trend will definitely continue. Because there are few implementable international laws regarding fresh water management, "there is a the risk of a 'race to the pumps' situation if pressure on water resources continues to build."[56] According to the Global Policy Forum, "More than 50 countries on five continents might soon be caught up in water disputes unless they move quickly to establish agreements on how to share reservoirs, rivers, and underground water aquifers."[56] Current concern, however, is probably most pronounced within countries of the Middle East. In 2011, Pakistan faced numerous conflicts because of disputes over irrigation, leading to the death of hundreds. That same year, a violent protest over water occurred in India. In the past year, both Afghanistan and Pakistan have witnessed attacks dealing with water supply. But the Middle East is not the only area stricken with water conflict. In 2013, numerous water issues arose in Peru and Brazil, where violent protests and police actions led to multiple deaths.[57]

To solve and avoid similar disputes in other international riparian zones, affected countries need to employ measures that encourage technological innovation and cooperation. Beyond that, world leaders have to develop cost-effective measures to increase fresh water availability and to control demand. They must also work to preserve water supplies through more efficient irrigation techniques, dams, and pipelines. When developing water policies, they must additionally realize that because of climate change, resources are never static. Some Middle Eastern and North African countries are already making efforts to mitigate the issue through constructing desalination plants; according to the University of Michigan, the plants have already helped 130 nations in both areas.[58] Fearing repercussions of climate change combined with water scarcity, countries in Africa "are set to apply innovative integrated approaches [such as improving their climate observatory operations] to strengthening their water, agricultural and energy sectors," as reported by the Daily Trust.[59] And despite protests, water-stressed governments in India and Mexico have invited corporations to privatize freshwater allocation to consumers. These cases suggest that as water scarcity increases, businesses and governments will take the lead, researching and implementing new water management processes, facilities, and technologies.

FOOD

The availability of food — the second resource under consideration — is tied to population growth, governance, and technology. From 2010 to 2012, the United Nations Food and Agriculture Organization estimated that almost 870 million were undernourished. Of these people, 852 million reside in developing countries.[60] This means nearly 13 percent of the world was undernourished, when the United Nations Food and Agriculture Organization conducted its study. Though in Asia, in the Pacific, in Latin American, and in the Caribbean the number of hungry people fell, the number escalated from 175 million to 239 million in Africa. In this region, nearly one in four people suffer from undernourishment.[61] In total, however, the number of hungry people worldwide has decreased, by over 150 million since 1990.[62] Although the world's agriculture does produce enough food to theoretically feed everyone, many people do not have access to the land or money needed to obtain proper nourishment. In crisis countries, a combination of low agricultural productivity, drought, poor distribution systems, regional conflict, and population growth has increased the demand for food aid. Such circumstances require donor nations to elevate production and employ more efficient distribution systems. Yet, recently, many afflicted countries have attempted to combat the hunger problem themselves. According to research conducted by the Institute of Development Studies, many low-income countries "are leading the charge."[63] Unfortunately, the study also found that a country's economic prosperity or growth does not correlate to its government helping to fight issues of hunger plaguing the nation. For example, as found by the study, Guatemala's government is currently the most committed to solving the issue, while countries in South Asia much wealthier than Guatemala do not see as much political involvement.

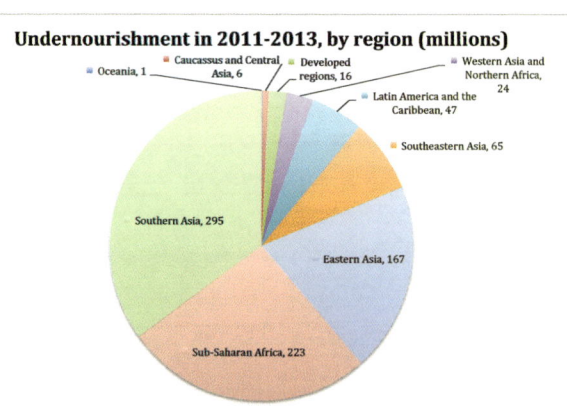

Source: Food and Agriculture Organization of the United Nations

Political instability has also been a root cause of famine in a number of developing countries. Wars and civil disputes have historically limited food availability. In some cases, governments have even restricted its own people's access to food as a scare tactic. Sri Lanka serves as a perfect example: "…several hundred Tamils recently demonstrated in the northern Vanni region against what they alleged to be an official government policy of restricting food supplies to the region," according to the article "Food Security and Political Stability in the Asia-Pacific Region."[64] Mitigating the disruption of supply lines and the politicization of food aid will certainly improve nutrition in a number of crisis countries. Similar to the water scarcity issue, studies have also shown that the hunger crisis has resulted in social unrest. For a more specific example, consider that a study from the New England Complex Systems Institute found an explicit link between violent protests in North Africa and in the Middle East in 2008 and 2011 and significant peaks in global food prices. As the study stated, "If food prices remain high, there is likely to be persistent and increasing global social disruption."[65]

Aside from governmental involvement, a combination of technology and increased market efficiency could serve to help alleviate the world's food crises in the near future. Companies have already boosted crop yields of a variety of food staples by engineering plants resistant to pests, droughts, and diseases. Scientists have also modified and supplemented common foods, such as rice, to include essential vitamins. Many people, however, remain skeptical that genetically modified food is the answer to the hunger crisis. Though GM crops are on the rise, a 2008 IAASTD report concluded that presently there are too many issues attached to GM foods for them to be of real use, especially considering much of the technology used to produce them is unregulated.[66] Nonetheless, the future of these crops could provide future potential benefits. Additionally, as more people become increasingly wealthy worldwide, food production will need to be expanded by 50 percent by 2030 to accommodate their change in tastes. No longer will these people will newfound wealth agree to subsist on rice and beans. Perhaps GM foods might provide an answer.

Those supporting the Doha Round of the World Trade Organization believe that though the answer to the hunger crisis lies in agriculture, it's not necessarily in agricultural engineering. Rather, the answer resides in reducing agricultural trade barriers, especially in the United States and the European Union. Started in 2001, the Doha Round's goal is to establish a reformed international trading network. Currently, many developing countries contend that farm subsidies in wealthier countries exacerbate food shortages and increase their dependency on assistance. Although the Doha Round is still occurring, it has reached some success. As stated by the World Trade Organization, "the July 2008 package is a stepping stone on the way to concluding the Doha Round. The main task before WTO members was to settle a range of questions that would shape the final agreement of the Doha Development Agenda."[67]

ENERGY

In addition to accessibility of water and food, energy availability is another ongoing and conventional business concern. The central question surrounding the management of fuel resources is not whether fossil fuels will persist in monopolizing the market, but rather whether alternative, renewable sources of energy will gain widespread acceptance. Though the 2013 International Energy Outlook found that, in addition to nuclear power, renewable resources are the world's quickest-growing energy sources, by 2040, fossil fuels will continue to dominate the market.[68] Power provided by fossil fuel sources is cheaply extracted but environmentally destructive. By 2040, the IEO predicts the global carbon emissions will have increased by nearly 50 percent or around a total of 45 billion metric tons. Some renewable, environmentally friendly energy sources, such as solar, hydro, and wind, have been implemented, but their market price remains significantly higher than conventional gas, oil, and coal energy resources. Additionally, some doubt that actively using these renewable energy sources is, in fact, environmentally friendly. For example, "Currently the EU has a set target of gaining 10% of its transport fuel from green sources by 2020; however, questions are being asked over whether the biofuels contributing to the achievement of this target are really leading to lower greenhouse gas emissions, or whether the drive to achieve the target is actually detrimental to the environment."[69] And though the IEO projects by 2040 both wind and solar energy will play a larger role in supply, these sources will still only represent a small portion of the world's overall energy consumption.[70]

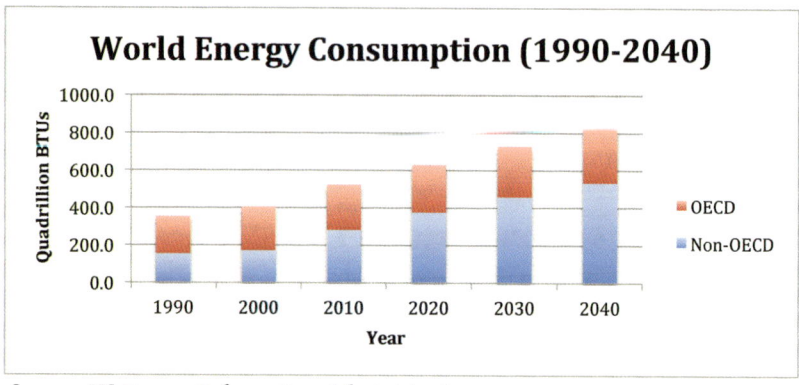

Source: US Energy Information Administration

Without any serious incentives to overturn the energy status quo, most industries will continue to rely on oil and gas, much of which comes from deep reserves in the Middle East. The investment to increase energy production by 40 percent by 2030 is estimated to require $26 trillion of investment in infrastructure. Furthermore, the energy consumption is anticipated to double by 2050. Who will provide the finances and what will occur if the investments are delayed? Moreover, the predominant oil and gas reserves are in the Middle East and in Russia. Given the political climate of the region, will the investments be made? In the near future, United States' industries may no longer rely on this Middle Eastern source of oil and gas. Until recently, many politicians, scientists, and the general public alike were greatly concerned with the United States' reliance on the Middle East and Africa for energy imports. This is, however, largely no longer the case, thanks to new technologies in drilling and alternative fuels. In fact, according to the IEO, "...America will surpass Saudi Arabia as the biggest oil producer in 2020 and become self-sufficient in energy by 2030..."[71] With this advantage, will the United States' interests in security of the Persian Gulf be reexamined? If the U.S. pulled out, the U.S. would then reap financial benefits, as U.S. taxpayers would no longer have to pay for a large military deployment, which potentially totals "a hundred bullion dollars or more in annual budget savings."[72] Will the financial benefits to the taxpayers justify the U.S. withdrawing as the policemen of the region? For other nations, namely the Arab oil states a part of the Gulf Cooperation Council, the United States' military withdrawal could have some severe repercussions. Who would take on the responsibility of policing the trade routes, including the Strait of Hormuz and Malacca, the entrance to the Red Sea and the Suez Canal, which are threatened by nations and inhabited by Somali and other pirates, and in politically tumultuous areas? Without the military support of the United States, will East Asian nations' militaries take on a larger role? And how will this new energy self-sufficiency affect the United States' global economic and foreign policy strategies? How will countries — particularly Russia & Saudi Arabia, two leaders in energy supply — respond to this new economic environment? Ultimately, what effects will the shifting energy dynamics have for other countries dependent on oil and natural gas resources?

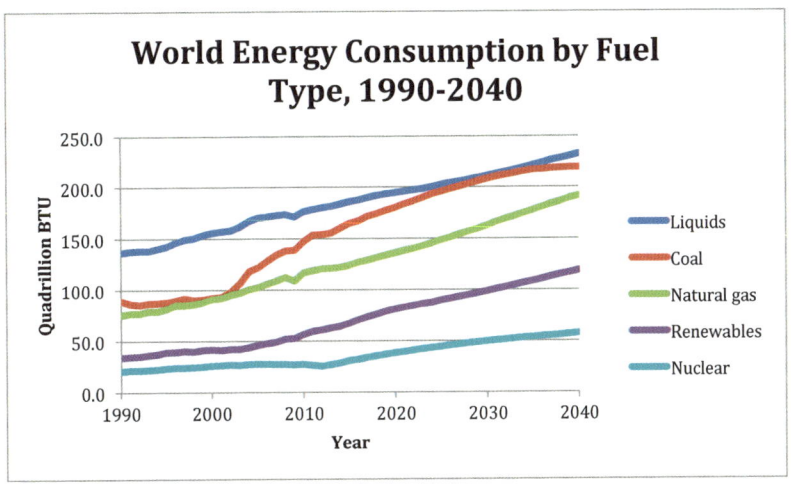

Source: US Energy Information Administration

Despite significant reserves in fossil fuels, companies and governments may still struggle to meet energy demands, especially in growing nations. According to the IEO, it is expected that developing countries in the near future will insist on their own portion of the world's energy. As further explained, "Of the nearly 300 quadrillion BTUs in added energy needed to meet global requirements between now and 2040, some 250 quadrillion, or 85%, will be used to satisfy rising demand in the developing world."[73] Of all the countries worldwide, during the next 30 years, China, which already currently consumes the most energy, is projected to utilize the largest energy share at 40%. This shift in energy consumption to developing countries is expected to result in turmoil, as there will be "intense competition for access to available supplies," as stated in the article "When will the Clean Energy Future We Dream of Actually Arrive."[74]

In the future, the regulation and availability of food, water, and energy will present many challenges and opportunities to businesses around the world. Good governance could make all resources more accessible, while advances in technology could help alleviate food and water shortages. The stability and security of the broader macroeconomic environment will depend on the success with which countries across the world can provide food and water to relentlessly expanding populations. Fossil fuels will continue to be in high demand, though it is possible that technological and political change could lead to increased reliance on alternative energy sources. The viability of commercial operations across the globe will depend on energy intensity, the price and efficiency of energy supplies, and the stability of energy supplies and prices. Business and community leaders should pay careful attention to trends in the availability of water, food, and energy to manage their resources more efficiently for the future. Additionally, it is expected that technological innovation propelled by the private sector will play an extremely important role in the degree to which humanity can improve its stewardship of food, water, and energy.

ENVIRONMENTAL DEGRADATION

CHAPTER FIVE

By Fariboriz Ghadar & Kathleen Loughran

During the 2012 United Nations Conference on Sustainable Development, also known as Rio+20, world leaders renewed many of the principles set forth under the 1992 United Nations Conference on the Environment. Because these leaders agreed that significant progress has not been made since 1992, they mainly reestablished their commitment to sustainable development — one that would not only help countries prosper economically and socially, but would also operate harmoniously with nature. Over 20 years ago, the World Commission on Environment and Development drew a link between the environment and economic and social prosperity. And, as found by the World Bank's 2003 World Development Report, the world's economy could grow significantly and poverty could be greatly reduced during the next 50 years — but only if governments mitigate hazardous strains on the environment.[75] Also, given public concern over air and water pollution and land degradation, companies that want to maintain an edge in their industry should follow environmental trends carefully.

Despite these reports and rising public concern, recently when countries have made development decisions, few have considered the environment.[76] As stated in "Environment for Development," "Environmental degradation is therefore undermining development and threatens future development progress."[77] According to the United Nations Environment Programme, the world's poorest nations are the ones that suffer the most from environmental degradation. Because their people rely so heavily on the land for life, they are inherently the most susceptible to environmental changes and disasters. Additionally, these people often live in physically exposed areas without financial security to adapt, making them especially vulnerable to the effects of climate change, according to the World Bank's 2010 World Development Report.[78] Many Least Developed Countries (LDCs) largely suffer from erosion, desertification, biodiversity loss, and deforestation, while more-developed, industrialized countries contend mostly with air and water pollution associated with manufacturing, fossil fuel use, and land conversion. With their recent rapid industrialization and urbanization, China, India, South Korea now sustain the majority of the world's carbon emissions.[79] In fact, because of voiced anger regarding China's air pollution in heavily populated cities, the government announced in late October that it would begin monitoring the effects of pollution on health. Additionally, Beijing released plans for dealing with extreme levels of pollution, including reducing the number of government cars on the road and closing schools.[80] Clearly, the industrialization of developing economies, combined with sustained growth in developed countries, will exacerbate worldwide environmental degradation and will continue to remain a concern for all nations.

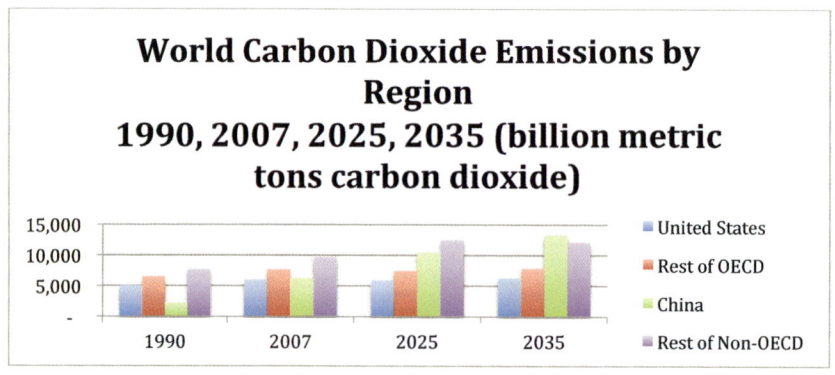

Source: http://www.eia.gov/environment/emissions/ghg_report/pdf/0573(2009).pdf

A global pursuit of stronger environmental protection and health standards intended to prevent this trend would increase regulatory and other costs for businesses. On the other hand, higher standards would stimulate investment in more environmentally sound manufacturing and production technologies. Moreover, as the United Nations Environmental Programme reported, "A study by eight corporate leaders on what business success would look like in the future concluded that it would be tied to helping society cope with challenges such as poverty, globalization, environmental decline and demographic change."[81] Concerned with the environmental and health effects of pollution, businesses, governments, and NGOs have already debated a range of possible policy responses to environmental degradation. Climate change, caused by fossil fuel conversion and the subsequent release of greenhouse gases (GHGs) into the atmosphere, has moved to the forefront of international discussions. In 1997 world leaders, looking for means to curb fossil fuel use, created the Kyoto Protocol. It wasn't placed into effect, however, until 2005. Signatories to the treaty hoped it would limit pollution while correcting inequities in the production of GHG.[82] Specific rules for implementation, called the "Marrakesh Accords," were not accepted until 2001 at COP 7 in Marrakesh, Morocco. Commitment to these rules lasted from 2008 to 2012. Then, in December of 2012, world leaders met in Doha, Qatar to draft an amendment, named Doha Amendment to the Kyoto Protocol. Parties hope "to reduce GHG emissions by at least 18 percent below 1990 levels in the eight-year period from 2013 to 2020."[83] Though GHG emissions have decreased in North America, where they used to soar, they have significantly increased in places like China, a country that now produces more GHG emissions than the United States and Canada combined.[84]

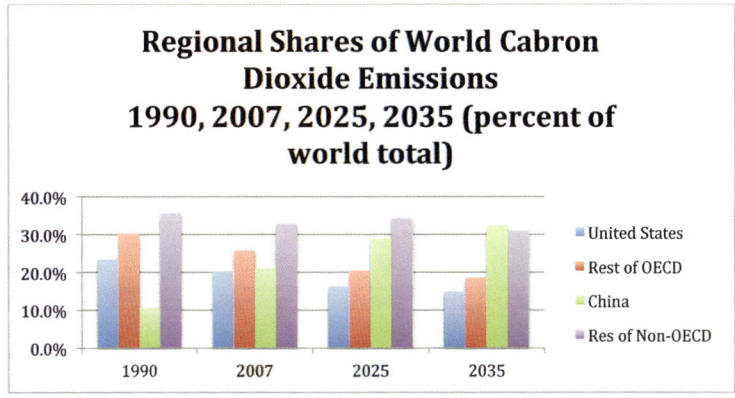

Source: http://si.conquestsystems.com/statistical/PdfMerge?id=nnzYx-EMN_3P2hjRT-Fs2CNHNxt88S8P7rGsPqKgTnwPYPfzyS4DR3beX-eAuEKiIL5noMOngcxPNwQ0Hk8OFErAI-chv2jTK5dOFrf3TPB73b-jN9b61fv554XLlPwsSW3xDPdrd4kHi31OlmOb35Ppjh1XZGBQP-6CLE5FNp9dBnFVlyVvAl5OvQ%3D%3D

Any international, regional or domestic plan to limit fossil fuel conversion in an effort to reduce GHG emissions, however, would result in hefty expenditures and thus would have considerable implications for businesses worldwide. In fact, according to the World Bank's 2010 World Development Report, to solve the problem, "Research and Development investments on the order of US$100 - $700 billion annually will be needed — a major increase in the modest $13 billion a year of public funds and $40 billion to $60 billion a year of private funds currently invested."[85] Additionally, policies, such as a carbon tax, or a carbon cap and trade system, outlined in Kyoto and other pollution control treaties, would fundamentally alter the way business is conducted.[86] Currently, some countries, such as those in the European Union, have already committed to a national action; others, like the United States, allow states the right to decide whether they wish to tax carbon.[87] Moreover, as stated by the article "What is carbon tax," the EU will eventually sanction countries that do not meet carbon reduction standards, thus limiting those countries ability to trade.[88]

Governments are also initiating plans to reduce air and water concentrations of sulfur dioxide, mercury, arsenic, and nitrogen oxide — compounds emitted mainly from coal power plants and manufacturing facilities. Many policymakers believe market-based solutions that specify a limited number of permits to pollute, bought and sold at market price, will be the most efficient method of reaching higher levels of environmental protection. Given this policy's popularity in Europe and its use in the United States with the nationwide Acid Raid Program and the regional Northeast NOx Budget Trading Program, corporations should now consider how to remain competitive in the face of tighter regulations enforced through "cap and trade" systems.[89] In addition to these systems, the United States has recently set other standards, such as doubling renewable energy resources and enforcing the highest fuel economy standards in its history. With these standards in tact, it is projected that by 2025 automobiles' efficiency levels will double, as well.[90] But President Obama doesn't want to stop there. Throughout his second term as president, he hopes to direct the EPA to enforce carbon pollution standards on power plants, which are the largest U.S. source of carbon emissions.[91] Also, by 2025, "The Department of Defense, the single largest consumer of energy in the United States, is committed to deploying three gigawatts of renewable energy on military installations."[92] Energy waste will continue to be cut in homes, businesses, and factories through the Better Buildings Initiative, and the Environmental Protection Agency will "encourage private sector investment in low-emissions technology by identifying and approving climate-friendly chemicals while prohibiting certain uses of more harmful HFCs."[93] This will certainly cause many businesses to have to change the ways in which they operate.

But climate change caused by GHG emissions is not the only environmental issue with which policymakers must contend, as water pollution is another huge problem. According to the UN, "Up to 90% of wastewater in developing countries flows untreated into rivers, lakes and highly productive coastal zones, threatening health, food security and access to safe drinking and bathing water."[94] Though improvements have been made to some industries' level of pollution, water pollution globally is still on the rise. As more countries develop, there are inherently more industries contributing to the problem, as industry adds approximately 300-500 million tons of heavy metals, solvents, and toxic sludge to the water system each year. Developing countries dump 70% of their untreated industrial waste into their waters, further polluting the usable water supply.[95] Industrial water use typically rises with country income, increasing from 10% of total water use for low and middle-income countries to approximately 59% for high-income countries. Projected estimates indicate that the annual volume of water consumed by industry will rise from 752 km3/year in 1995 to an estimated 1,170 km3/year in the year 2025.[96]

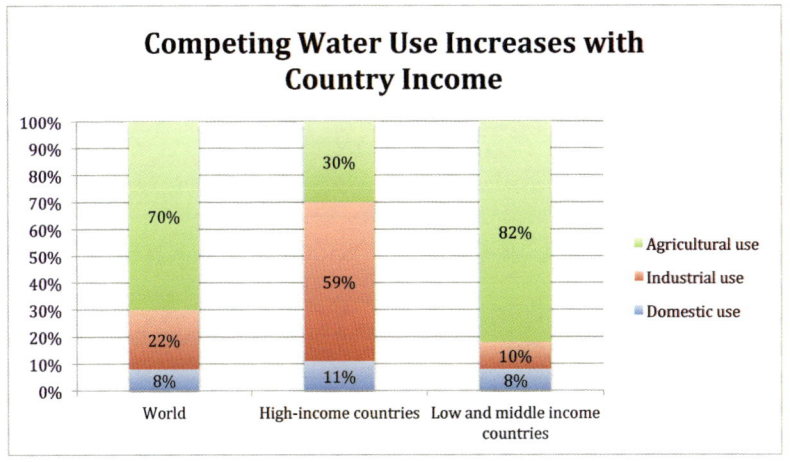

Source: http://www.unwater.org/downloads/Water_facts_and_trends.pdf

Though many developed countries have established systems to clean water used by industries, this is not the case for developing countries. As a result, industrial water in those countries is significantly more toxic. Although industry alone does not account for all water pollution, as agriculture is actually the biggest culprit, current trends of increasing corporate water use and pollution cannot continue unabated. Under the Executive Order 13514, "Federal Leadership in Environmental, Energy, and Economic Performance," the government is already forcing federal agencies to mitigate their contributions to the water pollution problem.[97] Given the scarcity of fresh water available for drinking and recreation, businesses can expect to face even tougher measures aimed at conserving and protecting existing water supplies.

Rising public concern over environmental pollution has generated greater corporate investment in the research and development of environmentally sound products. For example, a number of auto manufacturers, including Honda and Toyota, have developed fuel-efficient and fuel cell cars, which have the potential to lessen climate change.[98] Since 2000, when Ford and Air Products opened the first hydrogen station in North America, a number of stations have been opened worldwide. Though U.S.' plans have stalled for hydrogen highways, select European countries have either successfully developed such highways or have plans to do so. Clearly, businesses around the world are also exploring methods of creating and conserving energy and water. These examples of leading global corporations and countries preparing for the future indicate the importance attached to environmental policy by the business community.

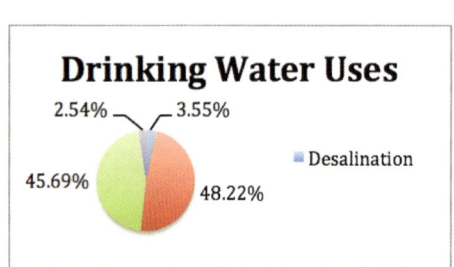
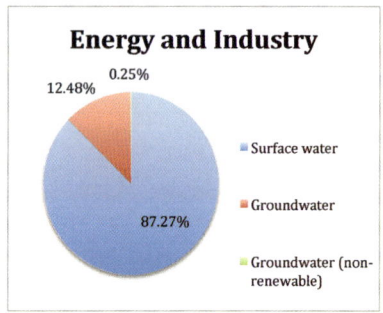
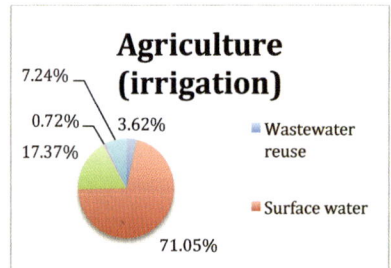
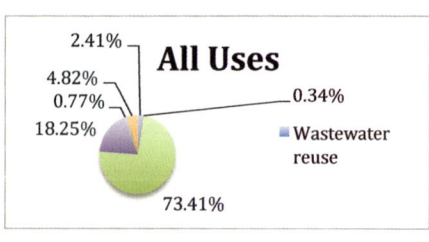

Source: http://webworld.unesco.org/water/wwap/wwdr/wwdr3/pdf/18_WWDR3_ch_7.pdf

Aside from air and water pollution, increased industrialization, commercial agricultural development, and urbanization has also raised the conservation issues of deforestation and biodiversity loss. For LDCs that lack the resources to develop and enforce environmental protection laws, these problems are more serious. Although in 2011, the Food and Agriculture Organization (FAO) showed declining rates of deforestation, about 13 million hectares of forest are still lost each year.[99] Because people have recognized the importance of these forests, some countries have implemented large-scale planting of trees, which has helped to mitigate the problem. According to the FAO, "The net change in forest are in the period 2000-2010 is estimated at -5.2 million hectares per year (an area about the size of Costa Rica), down from -8.3 million hectares per year in the period 1999-2000."[100] However, the efficacy of this tree planting has been contested by some, as a report titled "Understanding the impacts of Costa Rica's PES: Are we asking the right questions?" stated that this tree planting did not lower the deforestation rate.[101] Governments of some developing countries are now working to combine property rights and capitalism to help prevent environmental degradation while also promoting business development. Though regarded as controversial, countries such as Brazil and Australia have invited pharmaceutical and cosmetic corporations to mine biodiversity within their borders. The corporations hope to find new medicines, perfumes, and cosmetic products, while the host countries believe "bio-mining" may allow corporate development to augment biodiversity conservation. In fact, in Chile, it was recently discovered that through the use of bacteria, it might be possible to extract its large copper reserves without digging huge mine pits. More research, however, still needs to be completed to know the true effects of this development.[102]

Desertification and erosion, as well as pollution and deforestation, pose additional threats to environmental protection around the world. The gradual loss of soil productivity — resulting from land overuse, forest fires, excessive fertilizer use, and overgrazing — has become a worldwide problem. Recent estimates calculate the world has roughly 60 years of topsoil left.[103] According to an article published in TIME magazine, "…soil is being lost at between 10 to 40 times the rate at which it can be naturally replenished."[104] As a result of this degradation, it will be more difficult to grow food, resulting an estimated 30 percent loss within the next 20 to 50 years. Additionally, without proper soil, water cannot stay in the ground, and thus plants don't get their needed water and sea levels rise.[105] As found by World Information Transfer, over 250 million people in more than 100 countries are currently affected by desertification. Nearly 70 percent of Africa's land is at least semi-arid, and over $40 billion is lost each year because of desertification effects.[106] In China, more than a quarter of its land is degraded; however, efforts have been made to combat the problem. As reported by The Guardian, "In the five years to 2010, the authors estimated the area of desert had shrunk by an annual average of 1,717 square kilometers."[107] Still, worldwide, approximately 70% of the 5.2 billion hectares of dry lands used for agriculture are already degraded.[108] And, even though desertification is a natural occurrence, some studies have linked 70 percent of the degradation to human involvement.[109]

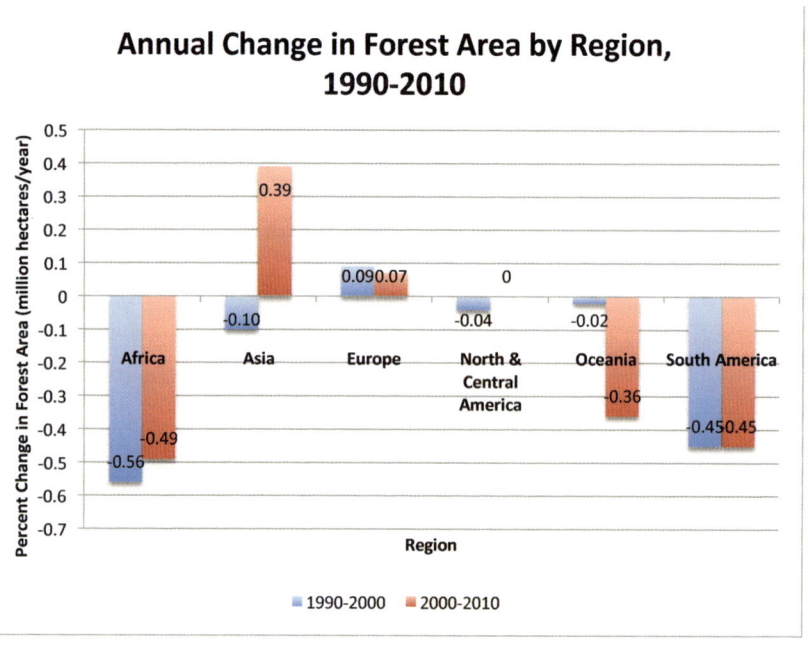

Source: http://www.fao.org/docrep/013/i1757e/i1757e02.pdf

These soil-loss problems threaten agriculture, husbandry, and water systems on every continent except Antarctica. Governments, multilateral institutions, NGOs and private corporations now partner to address the issues through poverty relief, through property rights implementation, and through technology transfers. Many countries facing desertification have already begun to rely on corporations to develop drought-tolerant plants, better irrigation processes, and new approaches to agriculture and husbandry. In South Korea, organizations and businesses have partnered to organize projects to help the problem. For example, the organization Future Forest began planting trees in 2006 along the Kubuchi Desert's border in an effort to combat strong winds.[110]

Though the international community must contend with a myriad of environmental problems, pollution, biodiversity loss, and desertification will prove to be the most challenging. Regulatory responses to these environmental issues will have far-reaching and extensive impact on businesses. At the same time, policymakers must recognize that environmental protection has historically been most successful when industry agrees and complies with conservation policies. Concerted efforts between businesses and governments, along with a nudge from concerned NGOs, can result in policies beneficial to environmental protection and to corporate viability.

ECONOMIC INTEGRATION

Source: http://www.radicalcartography.net

CHAPTER SIX

By Fariboz Ghadar & Kathleen Loughran

It could be argued that countries' economies have always been somewhat integrated through the trade of natural resources and goods. But, until recently, this is as far up the ladder of economic integration that countries have been able to proceed, and, even then, it has been mainly limited to developed countries. Though developed countries looked to developing countries for raw materials, they primarily traded with other developed countries. With the rise of multinational corporations (MNCs), however, this tectonic force has begun to shift. And the driving forces behind globalization — including faster communication, improved transportation, increased flows of goods and services, labor mobility, the proliferation of technology, and ever more rapid financial flows — have profoundly affected the world's economic landscape. Increased cross-border economic activity has contributed significantly to the overall growth of the global economy to approximately $84 trillion,[111] over four times its corresponding level in the mid-1970s. For these reasons, economic integration is on our list of global tectonic forces.

More or less, the story can be summed up in this simple phrase: The world is shrinking and interconnecting. Economic integration has led to the interaction and cooperation of companies and countries through trade in goods and services, the free movement of capital and foreign direct investment, and global manufacturing and supply chains. Because information, money, and investments now flow so rapidly, economies are becoming even more closely linked together. The most perceptible example requires a quick look at trends in the stock market, where diversifying your assets is the name of the game. People used to be able to easily diversify by investing in other countries' stock markets. As the world's economy becomes increasingly integrated, people can no longer use geography as a mechanism for diversification because now the stock market has begun to move in unison. Diversification now requires more thorough analysis and often investing across industries.

It should be no surprise that corporations and countries grow more rapidly when integrated. Each member of the European Union, for instance, finds ways to profit from the economic relationship. Spain and Portugal were granted membership in the European Community, the predecessor of the European Union, in 1986 to preserve their democratic societies. Prior to joining, their per capita income was 49 percent and 27 percent, respectively, of the income of the large European countries. By the turn of the century, the two countries saw those numbers rise to 67 percent and 38 percent — a significant increase due to economic integration.[112] Now, largely thanks to advancements in technology and increased knowledge dissemination, economic integration is no longer limited to the developed world. Through economic integration, much of the developing world has been able to grow very rapidly. For a more explicit example, consider that China has averaged about a 10 percent GDP growth rate each year since it became a more integrated and market-based economy in the late 1970s.[113] Additionally, the developing world is beginning to have stakes in the second feature of integration, foreign direct investment. Foreign direct investment, as the United Nations describes it, is "an investment made to acquire lasting interest in enterprises operating outside of the economy of the investor."[114] While inflows of foreign direct investment have traditionally flowed more to advanced economies than to developing economies, they flowed more to emerging economies than to advanced economies for the first time ever in 2012. In fact, four of the top five host economies were developing economies.[115] This recent trend in foreign direct investment shows that investors are placing more emphasis on the potential profits to be made in developing economies than in settling for the gains to be made in advanced economies. Among important recipients and investors of foreign direct investment over the past decade are the BRICS (Brazil, the Russian Federation, India, China, and South Africa), as foreign direct investment in these economies more than tripled from 2002-2012.

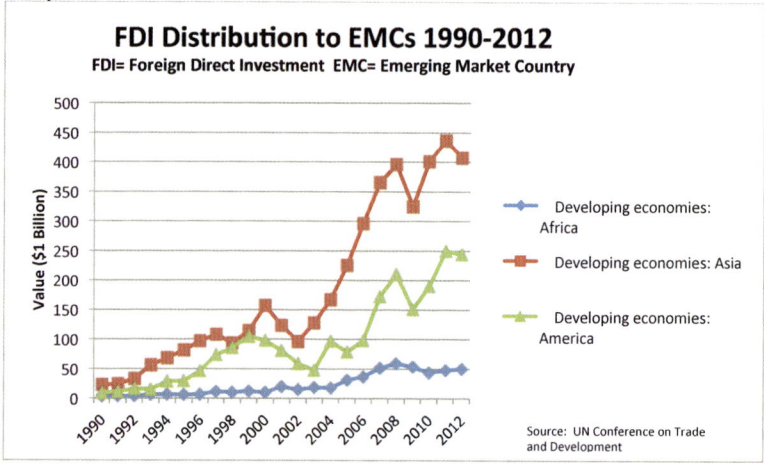

These new economies now have also assumed a key role in world trade sectors as diverse as traditional textile industries to more advanced high-technology manufacturing. No longer are they limited to trading raw materials with the developed world, as they have become manufacturing producers themselves — and this trend is expected to continue into the future. Manufacturing will remain the driver of growth and employment when nations are developing and continue to be a driver of innovation, trade, and production. "The new era will give manufacturing companies an opportunity to help their host economies in all of those areas; it will create high-skill jobs, particularly in design, big data, and other service roles…"[116]

But what is the implication of the participation of the developing world in manufacturing and in trade? We're beginning to see an increasingly global supply chain. As stated in a Center for Trade Policy Studies publication called "How Global Economic Integration Renders Trade Policy Obsolete," "The factory floor is no longer contained within four walls and one roof. Instead, it spans the globe through a continuum of production and supply chains, allowing lead firms to optimize investment and output decisions by matching production, assembly, and other functions to the locations best suited for those activities… The dramatic reduction in transportation and communication costs combined with wide-spread liberalization of trade, finance, and political barriers are all accomplices in what has been called 'the death of distance.'"[117] Centers for excellence are now global and integrated. The Boeing consortium is a perfect example of a company that collaborates with other entities in various countries. With its 787 Dreamliner, 45 companies from all around the world have a hand in each airplane's production. For example, the centre wing box is constructed by Fuji Heavy Industries in Japan; the raked wing tips are made by Korean Airlines Aerospace division; Alenia Aeronautica in Italy handles the horizontal stabliser and centre fuselage; and the final assembly is completed by Boeing Commercial Airplanes in the United States. By engaging in a global supply chain, Boeing is able to reap the benefits of real competition, share development costs, and ultimately create an airplane that is more efficient and technologically advanced. As the tagline states on its website, the 787 Dreamliner and Boeing are "flying into the future."[118] Boeing, however, is not the only company that has engaged in a global supply chain. Dell, GE Healthcare Worldwide, and Airbus are some of many other companies that have taken advantage of global supply chains. Even politically sensitive industries, like defense, have made use of global supply chains. For example, consider Lockheed Martin's F-35 Lightning II fighter plane, which is created through the use of people all around the world. Additionally, individual companies have increasingly expanded globally, leading to the globalization of products. For a more explicit example, consider the products of many luxury brands. Not only can you find the same purse from Louis Vuitton, a French company, in many stores worldwide, but you can also find knockoffs of its design in countries such as China.

Although we have begun to greatly witness the movement of capital, manufacturing, and products, we have only minimally seen the movement of people. Increasingly, though, we are starting to see the movement of people who are particularly skilled and well educated. Additionally, due to advancements in technology, the world's knowledge is becoming more integrated as people are able to more easily communicate and to share information across borders. And, as populations particularly in developed countries age, the movement of people will play an important role in the future. For instance, the United States is projected to experience a labor conundrum within the next decade when the retirement age of the youngest baby boomers (2019) coincides with when newborns from the era of the smallest American birth rate on record will join the workforce. To maintain or increase the level of American output, an influx of workers will be needed. It is estimated that 76 million baby boomers will retire by 2030, but only 46 million U.S.-born workers will have entered the workforce by then, leaving immigrants and the children of immigrants to fill the gap of the labor force.[119] Immigration of skilled and even unskilled labor will provide a competitive edge for countries that embrace these new workers. Countries like Canada, Singapore and Australia have already begun to attract skilled labor for their economic development and integration, and the United States and other countries should take note that skilled labor will become even more critical in the decades ahead.

Though economic integration is an imperfect process, the financial links between countries will grow stronger in the future. Since the 1994 Uruguay Round of WTO negotiations, developing countries have pined for greater access to markets. Similarly, developed countries have tried to advance agreements on the protection of investment and intellectual property.[120] Given the slow and contentious nature of WTO negotiations—the 2003 Cancun talks, for example, broke down over agricultural protectionism — many countries choose not to wait for multilateral resolutions.[121] Instead, many negotiate and enter into bilateral and regional trade agreements. The North American Free Trade Agreement (NAFTA) for instance, is one of an almost countless array of agreements connecting countries in what is now referred to as the "spaghetti bowl effect."[122] Though debate continues over whether regional agreements promote or hinder multilateral free trade, it is likely that countries will continue negotiating for greater market access in both regional and global trade forums.

Based on current trends, integration into the global economic system will remain a top priority for corporate and country leaders. Companies with assets abroad will monitor closely the economic vitality of their foreign affiliates. Exchange rate and financial crisis are direct results of capital market integration, and firms will therefore carefully track country indicators for signs of financial weakness. This will not be easy for commercial players like Boeing, which maintain operations around the globe. In order to respond to this global tectonic of economic integration, corporations will have to devise a constellation of new management strategies to track political developments and monitor the productivity of thousands of employees in any number of countries. Centers of excellence in many countries need to be developed and managed over time. As countries develop new talents and sources of expertise, new ones will appear and will need to be incorporated in the MNC's supply chains. Despite the risks associated with global integration, over the last 30 years the benefits of free trade, open capital markets, and international expansion have far outweighed the costs. A globally integrated economy where everyone depends on each other will likely make the world safer. This inherently plays into the changing nature of conflict, for countries will be less likely to declare war on other countries for fear of hindering the entire world's economy. In order for a global economy to be successful, however, some policy issues and regulations, such as taxation, trade regulations and investment policies, will need to be coordinated and negotiated. In any event, global integration demands more collaborative efforts occur. The free movement of goods, services, capital, and labor will continue to bring the world economies closer together and more integrated.

KNOWLEDGE DISSEMINATION

Source: Sage Ross

CHAPTER SEVEN

By Fariborz Ghadar & Kathleen Loughran

Knowledge — the production and dissemination of context-dependent information —plays an increasingly important role in the generation of wealth around the world. In this Third Wave economy, ideas and know-how are proving to be as valuable as the traditional factors of production: capital, land, and labor. In fact, according to an OECD report, "it is estimated that more than 50 per cent of Gross Domestic Product (GDP) in the major OECD economies is now knowledge-based."[123] Collecting and redistributing information, a way to leverage knowledge among industries, has increased business efficiency, enabling companies to make more informed decisions. Information sharing has helped end the duplication of effort, saving time and resources. Most organizations now prefer to share information with their stakeholders, clients, and suppliers through the Internet, helping them improve their overall business strategies and product offerings. The speed of knowledge dissemination has resulted in shorter product development cycles and has increased overall IT capability and capacity, with corresponding declines in the cost of hardware and transmission.

But the importance of knowledge dissemination to country and industry growth is not a new phenomenon. Rather, the rapidity in which it can be shared and transferred marks the greatest change. Historically, the transfer of knowledge has been a slow, arduous process. In the absence of technology, people would have to rely on their own personal inventions or on the sharing of knowledge through physical interactions. As such, it would take decades, if not centuries, for knowledge to spread. For a more specific example, consider the fact that the Chinese discovered how to make gunpowder possibly as early as 850 A.D., yet it wasn't until the silk trade route between Europe and the Islamic World was active in the 13th century that the science was transferred.[124] Then, with inventions aiding communication, such as the printing press and the telegraph, it became easier to preserve and to spread knowledge, leading to a quicker dissemination of new ideas and technologies both nationally and globally. Take the invention of the television as an example. The first electronic television picture came into existence in 1927 in the United States.[125] Less than 30 years later, the technology was active in countries like South Korea.[126] Over the years, people's consumption of this new technology has also rapidly increased. Though Guglielmo Marconi was awarded the patent in Britain for the radio in the late 1890s, it wasn't until the 1930s when the majority of American households became equipped with the device.[127] Comparatively, it only took about 20 years for the television industry to sweep the American market.[128] Now, Apple can release a new version of its iPhone 5 and sell 9 million phones in just one launch weekend, as was the case in its most recent release of the iPhone 5S and 5C.[129] And this consumption is not limited to the developed world: "Less than 30 years after Ameritech phoned Bell's grandson in America's first commercial cellular call, an astounding 158 out of 200 countries the World Bank monitors have passed the threshold with mobile phones — including countries such as Senegal, where the average income is only $5 per day."[130]

In order for this technology to exist for people to consume, however, there obviously has to be people capable of developing such devices. If we look back in history, traditionally one country initially becomes the forerunner of a certain industry because its workers are skilled in that area. As an example, motivated by the prospects of profit, many of Britain's population eagerly sought answers to make life simpler, which ultimately led to the shaping of the world's first Industrial Revolution. During this time, the United Kingdom developed many inventions, such as Thomas Newcomen's 1712 creation of the steam engine. Additionally, machinery that dramatically sped up the process of spinning and weaving wool was executed, allowing Britain to become the heart of the wool industry for many years.[131] Recognizing the value of having people competent enough to continue to create such inventions, Britain placed an increased emphasis on education during the Industrial Revolution. New school systems were developed, and the proportion of children in schools increased.[132] Largely because of this high level of education, Britain has been able to retain significant power in the world. Yet, England has not been the only country to recognize the value in educating its populace. Other historical examples illustrate its importance, such as the growth of Germany and Japan after World War II. Two countries that arguably suffered the most during the war were able to prosper soon after because they placed an emphasis on educating the younger generation. Moreover, a look at the United States' little house on the prairie school systems can explain why the country achieved such greatness during the late 19th/early 20th century. For a more current example, consider the development of Silicon Valley in the United States. Although there are multiple theories regarding the establishment of this prosperous region in the United States, one element remains consistent: it required the presence of brilliant, innovative people with the knowledge to create such inventions as a programmable computer chip and a general-purpose integrated circuit. If these United States' workers had not been equipped with this knowledge and education, however, it is conceivable that Silicon Valley, at least the one in the U.S., would not exist in its current form.

Additionally, with the lapse of time, people in other countries begin to acquire similar knowledge and skill sets, allowing them to no longer be reliant on the original source. Such was the case with the British wool industry; other countries have since been able to develop their own machinery and have gladly resorted to using it. And a similar story has happened in Silicon Valley, where technology firms have actually actively sought out people in foreign cities, such as Bangalore, for their knowledge and skills.[133] Microsoft founder Bill Gates recognizes the trends in knowledge dissemination and illustrates how geography no longer trumps talent in the world of globalization. "Thirty years ago if you had a choice between being born a genius on the outskirts of Bombay or Shaghai or being an average person in Poughkeepsie [N.Y.], you would take Poughkeepsie because your chances of thriving and living a decent life there, even with average talent, were much greater," he said.[134] Today, Gates would choose to be a genius in China over an average person in rural New York because the world has become increasingly flat. A similar thought was mentioned by Thomas Friedman, who also said "you can now innovate without having to emigrate."[135]

China is one nation taking advantage of the benefits of globalization, capitalizing on its vast source of knowledge workers and investing in improving education, especially in math and science. The city of Dalian, located about an hour by plane northeast of Beijing, exemplifies how rapidly China's cities are attracting businesses as knowledge centers rather than as manufacturing hubs. Leading companies including GE, Microsoft, Dell, SAP, Sony and Accenture have begun doing business there, setting up backroom support and new software research and development centers.[136] A clear-cut example of how seminal proper education is to a country's development can be illustrated with a comparison of China to many other developing countries. In the 1990s, China's exports grew faster than many other countries because of what China was doing right. China's advantages in education, privatization, infrastructure, quality control, mid-level management, and the introduction of new technology helped the country find success and grow, while others fell behind. The Chinese government continues to place heavy emphasis on research and development, creating greater public awareness for innovation and reforming financial and tax systems to promote growth in cutting-edge industries. What are controversial areas of investigation in some countries, such as stem-cell research and gene therapy, face minimal regulation in China. China is also actively developing its software, semiconductor and energy industries, including renewable energies such as hydro, wind, and solar power.[137]

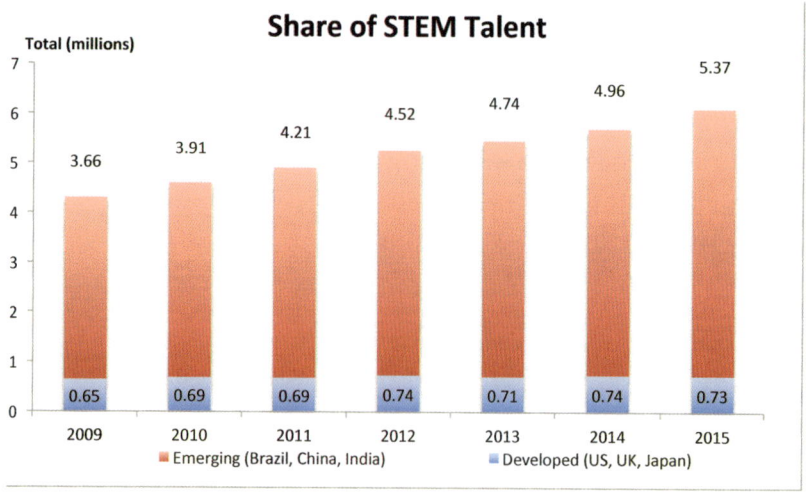

Source: http://www.accenture.com/SiteCollectionDocuments/Accenture-No-Shortage-of-Talent.pdf

Realizing that science and technology are at the forefront of the modern economy, China implemented efforts to educate young people in these fields to promote growth and economic development for the nation. Through their science and technology policy implemented in 1995, Chinese leaders established a number of basic principles and goals. Among these principles is the mission: "Respect knowledge, respect talent, and create an environment favorable for people's exhaustive playing of their roles and cultivating and bringing up new talent."[138] This notion sums up the importance of knowledge in the world of globalization, and it explains the mindset that has allowed China to rise to the top as a major player in the knowledge industry. Moreover, by 2020, the Chinese government hopes to have established an innovation-centered economy, according to a paper by Joel R. Campbell.[139] In following this strategy, China has taken steps to realize its nation's knowledge potential by investing heavily in education. In 2004 the central treasury of China appropriated more than 10 billion yuan (roughly $1.2 billion) for compulsory education in rural areas, up an incredible 70 percent from the previous year. As a result of the increased funding for education, more than 2 million illiterate people received education and about 24 million students from impoverished areas have received free textbooks.[140] Additionally, boarding schools in western rural areas were built, and thousands of ramshackle secondary and elementary schools were renovated. Now these Chinese students, even if they are poor, have a responsive government giving them the tools to compete in the globally integrated world.

Moreover, the government shows no signs of stopping this support. In fact, quite the opposite is happening. In early 2013, it was reported that, "China's annual fiscal expenditure on education has surpassed 2 trillion yuan."[141] According to Yan Weifang, director of the Education and Economy Research Institute of Beijing University, the Chinese government has further plans to continually increase access to education, especially in rural, poor areas. Through the Ministry of Education, the Chinese government has also funneled money into developing research programs at the university level. As stated by Campbell, "Universities now perform about forty percent basic research and thirty percent of applied research," further helping to train and educate young minds. China's success has been evident in recent years. A talented knowledge pool and cheaper labor force have encouraged a number of companies to invest in projects in China and to set up companies there. By 2001, 400 of the Forbes 500 companies had invested in more than 2,000 projects in Mainland China.[142]

But China isn't the only country that has recently realized the importance of educating its populace. India is also emerging as a world leader in knowledge management due to globalization's impact on the speed and ease with which people share information. Like China, India's government regards education as a top priority. According to an article titled "Linking Funding and Quality to Improve Higher Education in India," "India's higher education system is one of the world's largest, enrolling nearly 22 million students in more than 46,000 institutions."[143] Additionally, a large percentage of the nation's wealth is invested in education, as the country, through private and public sources, spends more than the United States or Korea do.[144] It is worth noting, however, that the education system does have some persistent flaws because it is rather unorganized. Although there is a clear investment on the government's part, the sheer size of India's population has presented difficulties. Hopefully, however, the government's recent 12th Plan, which "seeks to alight Central government investment with that of State governments," will help to "align new capacity with demand."[145]

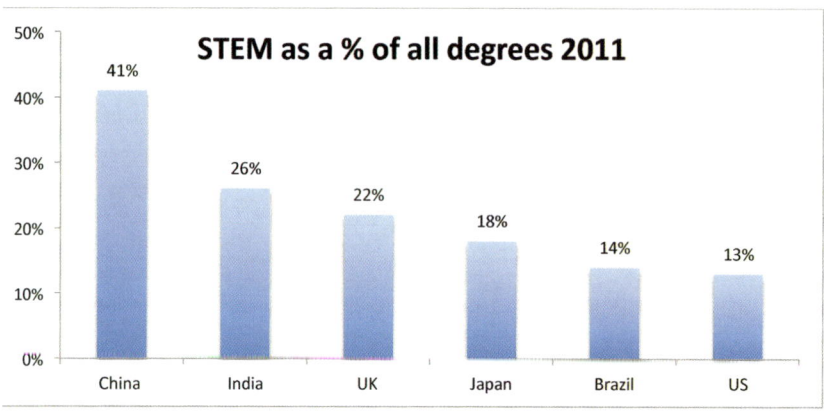

Source: http://www.accenture.com/SiteCollectionDocuments/Accenture-No-Shortage-of-Talent.pdf

India's commitment to educating its people particularly in science and technology has roots back to 1951 when Jawaharal Nehru, India's first prime minister, set up the first of seven Indian Institutes of Technology. Since then, hundreds of thousands of Indians have competed to attend and graduate from these prestigious schools. Already the world has seen the incredible results this emphasis on science and technology has had on the Indian economy. Revenues from the IT industry in India exceeded $100 billion in 2012,[146] and Nasscom predicts they will reach $225 billion by 2020.[147] It's safe to say that without Indian workers, Silicon Valley wouldn't be what it is today. Indian engineers have been coming to the United States in increasing numbers since the early 1970s. High-tech companies need people desperately, and U.S. engineering schools simply don't produce enough graduates to fill the specialized jobs the high-tech industry creates. In addition, many corporations claim that the engineers U.S. schools produce typically aren't as talented as those from India. (Bear in mind that Indian immigrants have graduated from schools that make Harvard and the Massachusetts Institute of Technology seem easy to get into by comparison).[148] With a population exceeding 1 billion in India, the rigorous competition to gain entry into these schools has provided the country with a rich source of people educated in science and technology. The IT work these Indians participated in helped them develop relationships with a number of large companies in the United States and led to the burgeoning Bangalore, India's very own Silicon Valley. Home to companies such as Microsoft, IBM, Goldman Sachs, Hewlett-Packard, and Texas Instruments, Bangalore has become a hub for knowledge workers. Companies such as these invested vast sums of money in bandwidth to connect Indian brainpower to American companies. The connections the IT workers made, coupled with the fact that India was now plugged into the global business society, led to tremendous opportunity for Indian knowledge workers.[149]

Though other developing countries have notably been more resistant to globalization and to knowledge dissemination, all countries will need to increase investments in higher education. A December 2002 World Bank report warns that developing countries will need to close the knowledge gap, even though many of these states lack the education systems and technological infrastructure to be competitive in a knowledge-based economy.[150] Additionally, to remain competitive, they will need to encourage advancements in tertiary education with the goal of increasing the availability of skilled labor and productivity. While countries and companies stand to benefit from the ease at which information can be shared, governments and corporations are just beginning to learn how to manage and protect knowledge, in this technology-driven, increasingly interconnected world. For instance, businesses that facilitate the creation of new technologies find that patents on information are difficult to obtain on the international level, where piracy and counterfeiting pose serious threats to specific industries. With the flattening trend of globalization also comes the realization that any open landscape requires the judicious placement of a few fences and gates. The United States is relying on patent, trademark, copyright, and trade secret laws, as well as confidentiality procedures and contractual provisions, to protect proprietary technology and brands. However, circumstances outside our control can pose a threat to intellectual property rights. For example, effective intellectual property protection may not be available in every country in which a firm's products and services are distributed, or the efforts taken to protect proprietary rights may not be sufficient. In addition, protecting intellectual property right is costly and time consuming. Technology and economic transformation are outpacing international legal institutions, and governments must work with corporations to establish more functional mechanisms for safe guarding investment in intellectual property.

The massive effort that connected the world via the Internet coupled with the increased availability and accuracy of information online has led to significant developments in the way global society functions. This rapid technological change and this emphasis on intellectual property are causing a winners-take all kind of environment. While this sometimes can be economically advantageous, it does come with a concentration of wealth by the knowledge producers. And this will likely become an issue as we move forward in the next decades to come. Competition for knowledge workers will continue to increase, as location becomes less important and personal knowledge and ability become paramount. Additionally, as economies of industries and countries specializing in technological advancements continue to boom, we can expect to knowledge to become increasingly paramount. According to an OECD report, "Output and employment are expanding fastest in high-technology industries, such as computers, electronics and aerospace."[151] Thus, governments will be forced to address the need for education, especially in the fields of science and mathematics. Companies will need to adapt, to share information among clients and suppliers, and to take advantage of labor wherever it is most qualified and profitable. Furthermore, countries and companies will need to develop ways to manage and protect their knowledge- and technology-based economies.

INFORMATION TECHNOLOGY

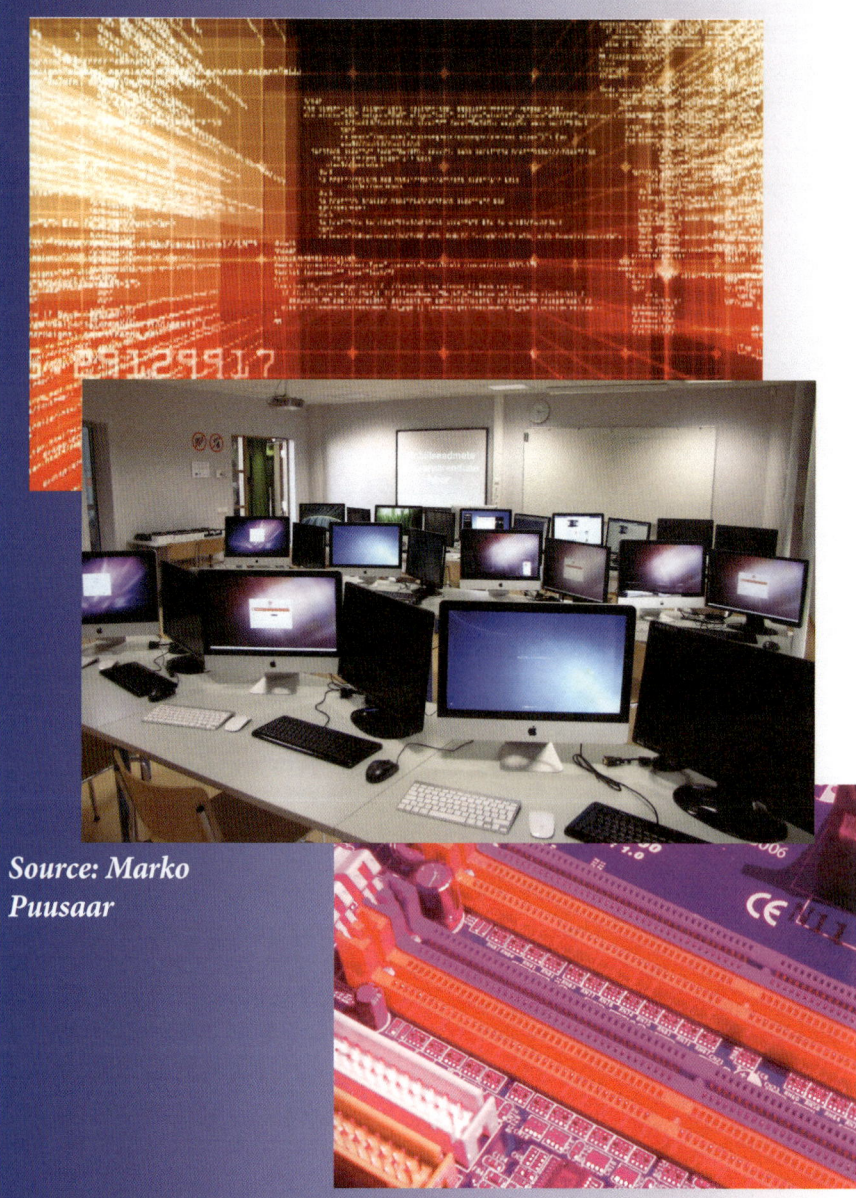

Source: Marko Puusaar

Note: Chapter originally published in Industrial Management

CHAPTER EIGHT

By Fariborz Ghadar & Kathleen Loughran

In less than half a century, the field of Information Technology (IT) has developed from one housed on huge stationary computers called IBM 360s, kept in air conditioned rooms and monitored by computer experts, to small mobile devices, like an iPhone, that can be used easily by virtually everyone in almost any location. Despite this unprecedented growth, this technological tectonic force is still expected to see major change in the near future. These advancements will inherently shape the world's future global business climate.

In recent decades, IT has already deeply altered how people live, work, learn, and interact with one another. While people used to have to wait for an available phone line to call each other to communicate on home telephones, people are no longer confined by the whims of others or by a cord in their house. They can now easily text each other's mobile devices and can even find out one another's location thanks to the advent of technologies like Foursquare. According to an article written by Samuel Greengard, a "tsunami of change is [currently] washing over IT organizations. The introduction of iPads and iPhones, social media, big data, and cloud computing have unleashed profound changes that far exceed the impact of each of these devices or systems alone."[152] Technology has allowed for a more competitive market simply because it gives greater access to information to more people. In the old days, for example, a cocoa farmer in West Africa would be forced to accept prices offered by European traders. Now, on his phone, he can look up how much chocolate sells for in London and demand a higher wage. Through the use of wireless technology, more people, especially those in rural areas, are gaining access to the Internet. As of 2012, nearly 35 percent of people worldwide used the Internet, representing a 566.4 percent growth since 2000.[153] And as the industry continues to expand, this number will only increase, thus furthering opportunities for businesses worldwide. But knowledge provided by the Internet extends beyond the cocoa farmer. On a broader scale, it has allowed companies to access new markets armed with information about demographics, cultures, tastes, preferences, and disposable incomes — ultimately allowing them to tailor their services and products to consumers. Customization will become the buzzword of industries where it hasn't already taken hold. As stated by Greengard, "Over the next few years, the role of IT will change further as the consumerization of IT marches forward and cloud computing provide more powerful ways to manage everything from infrastructure to enterprise application."[154] Already, IT has provided the capability for businesses to conduct market niche analysis. With it, businesses can track consumers' preferences, needs, habits, and desires. Through consumers' own engagement with IT, companies like Groupon can better appeal to their target markets. Say, for example, you're visiting a new city on a business trip; not only will Groupon be able to recommend hotels, but it also might supply a coupon to a nearby Indian restaurant because it knows you like Indian food. Or, take for example, your Facebook page. Ever notice how advertisements featuring pictures of clothes you clicked on days earlier appear on the side of your screen, subtly reminding you how much you loved that blouse?

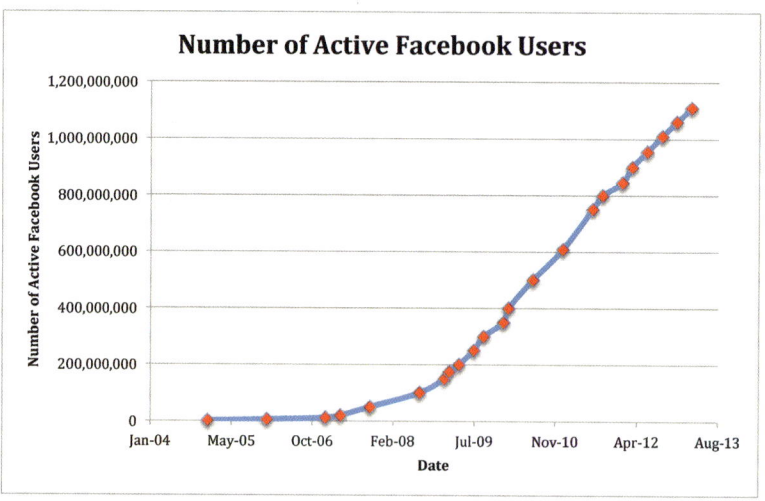

Source: http://news.yahoo.com/number-active-users-facebook-over-230449748.html

But, in general, where is this industry heading, especially because it has already seen such tremendous growth? Will it continue to have a major impact on the worldwide economy and global business environment? Simply put, the answer is yes. Because the commercial capabilities of the IT industry have only recently been tapped, many argue we are still in the young stages of this IT revolution. As early as 2020, Forrester Research expects the industry to look almost entirely different.[155] Not only will our devices be communicating with us, like the Groupon app does on phones by offering coupons at local businesses, but they will also operate self sufficiently. Take, for example, a car. Already GPS systems have been installed in many, and some cars even have the capability of being able to parallel park with minimal effort from the hand of the driver.[156] Thus, the future will see cars that no longer require the presence of a driver. In turn, what will that mean for the taxi industry, if people can simply call upon a robotic car? Additionally, there will no longer be a need for downtown parking lots if cars can drive themselves, so what will this mean for city planning? As both industries advance, the IT industry will continue to merge with the robotics industry, and futuristic cars won't be the only end result. Overall, according to a study produced by McKinsey Global Institute, as the mobile internet expands into emerging markets it — along with "the automation of knowledge, things such as computerized voices… and the 'Internet of things,' such as embedding sensors in physical objects to monitor the flow of products through a factory" — is expected to be worth at least $1 trillion each.[157] Therefore, devices with the ability to communicate with other gadgets, such as a refrigerator alerting a computerized system in grocery stores that you're short on yogurt, are no longer confined to the pages of science fiction novels.

Thanks to projected advancements in technological tools easy to acquire and to use, Forrester expects businesses to become even more self sufficient, resulting in smaller, more strategic IT departments. Technology can help companies in a number of ways, but it can also hurt those who do not take the time to assess what technologies will fit best with their mission. There are fundamental rules of business that cannot be ignored for flashier products. Employees need to be trained to use a new technology and understand how to employ the vast array of programs available to them. This changing dynamic will also have an affect on many businesses' individual IT departments. Because it will be necessary that most employees have general IT knowledge, the individual departments will thus most likely be streamlined, but also they will need to be more innovative. Greengard's article further explains, "To be sure, those that cling to the command and control model of the past are destined to face severe turbulence. Today, success hinges on a lean, agile, flexible and intrapreneurial IT model that's inextricably linked to business needs… In this upside down post-PC world, risk must be viewed as a friend and change as a potential competitive advantage."[158]

The IT revolution, however, won't just lead to companies better educating their employees, but it will also spark greater worldwide access to education. In fact, IT has the potential to completely revolutionize the current paradigm of education. With newfound organizations, such as Coursera, people will no longer need to attend universities to receive an education. Though courses like these are currently free and don't offer a degree, they eliminate the barrier to entry by providing nearly anyone access to some of the world's best educators. And, in the future as these courses become increasingly popular, we can expect to see a shift to this structure of education. All of this means education is going to globalize and to be much more readily available, thereby providing a real opportunity to the developing world. In fact, by 2020, Rwanda hopes to transition into a knowledge-based economy, presenting future opportunities for investors and businesses.[159] Thanks to this newfound knowledge and other capabilities provided by IT, this revolution will continue to influence economic development. Economies such as Hong Kong, Singapore, and Taiwan have benefited tremendously from the manufacture and sale of IT products. According to World Economic Forum's Global Information Technology 2013 Report, "digitization has a measurable effect on economic growth and job creation. In emerging markets, a comprehensive digital boost could help lift over half a billion people out of pov-

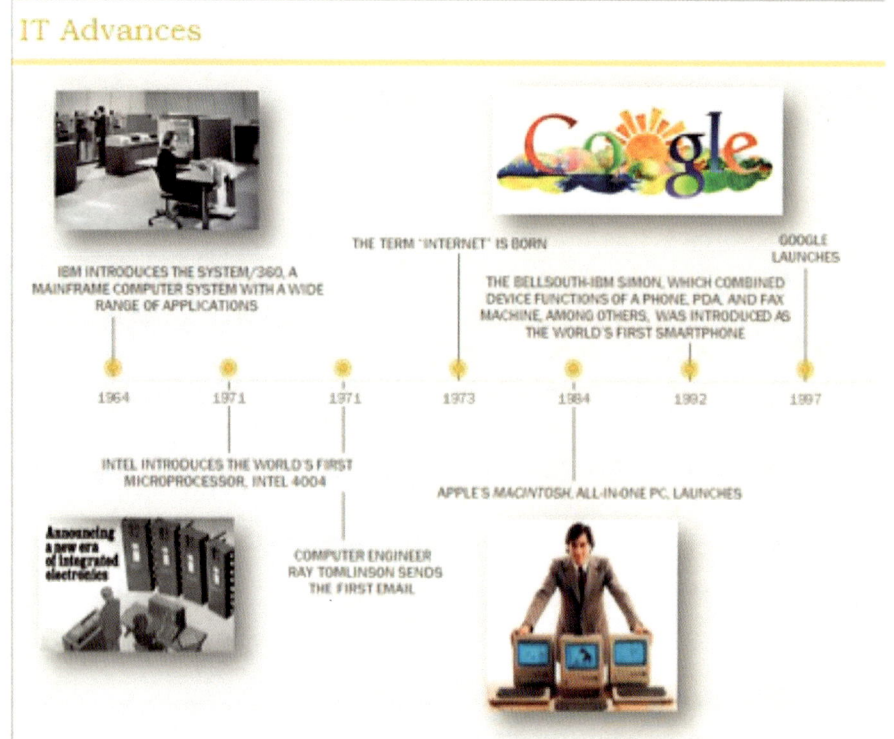

IT Advances

erty."[160] More explicitly, it found that, in the past two years alone, over $190 billion has been generated because of digitization.[161] Future growth could happen in Latin American countries that place an emphasis on education and innovation. Latin America's internet market could grow exponentially as countries deregulate their telecom industries, pursue developing IT markets, and adopt new technologies.[162] In fact, e-government has recently improved the lives of many people living in Latin America. For example, as stated in WEF's report, "In Panama, entrepreneurs used to need five days to set up a company. Now, thanks to PanamaEmprende, they can do it in 15 minutes."[163] Countries such as Argentina, Mexico, and Brazil will also present investors with vast opportunities.

Even though IT developments can stimulate economic growth, they do lessen individuals' and companies' access to privacy. Though we might find it cool that Google Earth can easily pinpoint and draw up where we live, consider what that means for our security if technology is publicly available for people to diagram unknown locations. Therefore, as public services adopt IT, they must protect individual privacy and ensure

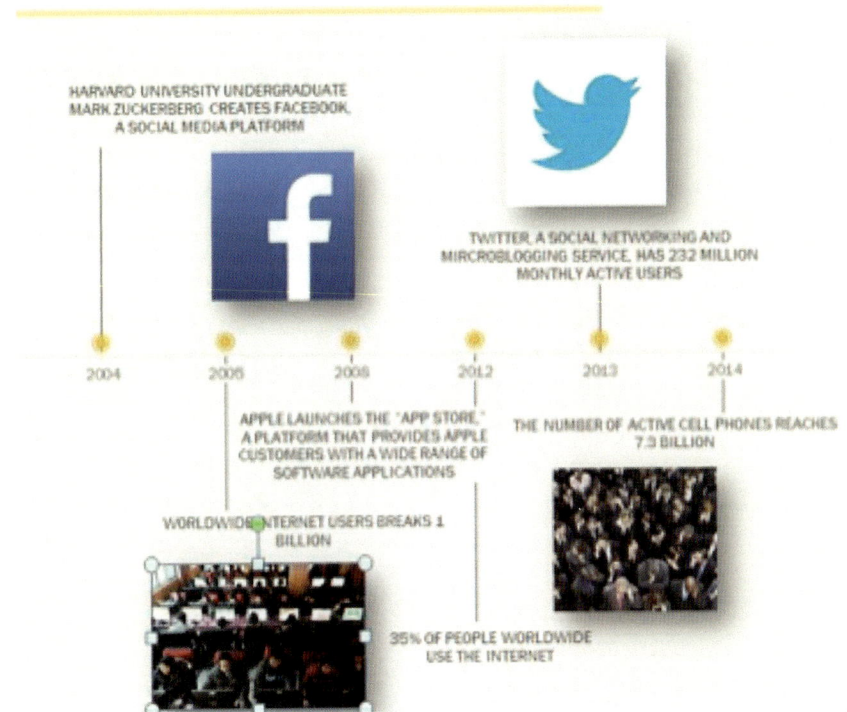

national security. For example, as more countries implement electronic voting, they will need to meet a host of security, privacy, and equity requirements. Internet hacking is now a federal offense in the United States, and it is likely that over time federal regulations and laws will develop to meet the demands imposed by advancements in and the adoption of new information technologies. Privacy issues are not only important because of Internet hacking, but also because they will be the growing focus of attention as an increasing amount of data on individual behavior is collected. Consider as an example a common trip to the doctor's office wherein all your medical history is recorded electronically. A technologically savvy individual could hack into your files and acquire all of your information. Though this would amount into a HIPPA violation and a million-dollar lawsuit, in the end, what would that really do? In the future, how are people going to protect that information? And who is going to take on that responsibility — the individual, the doctor's office, the government? Currently, most American companies regulated themselves. If companies make the choice to stop self-regulation, they will most likely face government imposed regulation as a concerned and worried public tries to prevent identity and information theft. As consumers, we will ultimately become more aware than ever before about who has our information and how it is being used. Are we prepared to live in a world where, because of the Patriot Act, security cameras, point-of-sale data collection, ATMs, and state-controlled camera in public places, our movements can literally be tracked hour by hour? As we adopt IT into all aspect of our daily life, there are sacrifices to personal privacy to be made. Nonetheless, where IT goes in the future will continue to shape the way society interacts, education reaches people, governments operate, and businesses function. It is now and will continue to be a crucial global tectonic.

ROBOTICS

Source: Sony_Qrio_Robot.jpg: Dschen Reinecke
derivative work: Jorgebarrios

CHAPTER NINE

By Fariborz Ghadar & Carl Boswell

On December 8th 1980, an imposing and resourceful robot dominated the cover of TIME Magazine alongside the headline "The Robot Revolution." At a time when home phones and word processors still reigned supreme, the world's population was already embracing the robot revolution. The issue's feature story referred to Chrysler's new automated 145-acre factory in Detroit, indicating the revolution had already begun.[164] Over two decades later, on January 25, 2004, the Mars rover Opportunity entered Mars' atmosphere to begin its 90 day mission of exploring the planet's landscape.[165] Ten years later Opportunity still operates and collects data for the NASA mission center back on Earth. In the years since the 1980 TIME Magazine cover landed on Americans' doorsteps, robotics has significantly grown. It is changing our society with galvanizing swiftness.

Source: http://marsrovers.jpl.nasa.gov/gallery/artwork/rover-1browse.html

While the NASA mission represents a significant milestone for human achievement in space, robotics is changing business on this planet as well. Growth predictions place industrial robotics as a quickly developing field. There were more than 1.2 million robots working in industrial placements in the world in 2013, approximately one robot for every

5,000 people according to Marshal Brain, author of Robotic Nation and founder of How Stuff Works.[166] Our society is not new to innovation; we have endured multiple booms in industrialization spanning from the production of the cotton gin, allowing for increased cotton production, to the innovative assembly line concept on the part of Henry Ford. The majority of the roles marginalized in the past were typically labor-intensive occupations.

Workplace mechanization has impacted all types of industries, from apparel to automotive. According to a 2013 Bloomberg report, automotive assembly line wages in China rose from $2,425 to $6,750 from 2005 to 2012.[167] In an attempt to tackle the rising costs of labor, Chinese manufacturers have begun to use industrial robots. These companies have the support of the local government, which is examining a rollout to invest over $80 billion into local factories over the next five years. In an industry where overcoming governmental hurdles and regulations is a major step to moving forward with robotics, this aide is welcomed. According to the International Federation of Robotics, in the 21st century, China has maintained the "world's fastest-growing market for industrial robots."[168] The German association predicts China will overtake Japan as the top purchaser of robots by 2016.[169] This regional trend is mirrored by shifts to mechanized platforms in factories all around the world, including the United States.

Robotic Advances

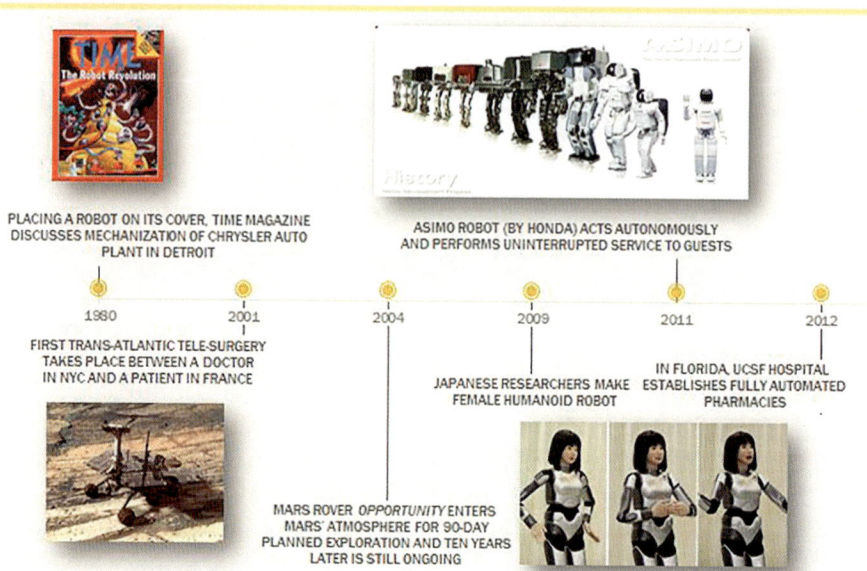

The newest mechanization phase places us in unfamiliar territory; a terrain in which all jobs, including the historically cerebral and stable vocations, are greatly affected. In 2012 the UCSF Medical Center instituted automated pharmacies at two UCSF hospitals, which greatly reduced interaction between physician and pharmacist.[170] In addition to pharmacy management, robotics is redefining the future of medical surgery. Remote surgery, or telesurgery, is a medical procedure performed without the doctor physically present. The first transatlantic surgery took place in 2001; while a patient lay in the operating room in France, her doctor acted in New York City, 4,000 miles away. With reduced physical limitations for doctors, the future possibilities are numerous. Rural patients and trauma cases can be treated with little delay. Additionally, surgeons will be able to see images previously difficult to obtain and they will be able to access the body with less invasive procedures.[171] Already, these new technologies, which allow for higher degrees of surgical precision and decreased invasiveness, have reduced patient recovery times.[172] The far reaching implications of robotics in the medical field will require changes in the way medicine is taught, patients are treated, and recovery is managed. This field is still in its infancy and only time will tell how expansive and feasible medical mechanization will become.

Shifting from the technologically advancing operation rooms of the hospital to the kitchen in one's home, robotics and automated appliances

will be ever-present features of the future. Imagine owning a refrigerator that knows precisely what you have placed within it. The Samsung RF 4289HARS does just that, but this cool gadget arrives at your doorstep with a steep price tag in excess of $3,000.[173] While consumers marvel at the innovation, the prices are prohibitively high. This fact showcases the evolution that most new breakthroughs undergo. Technologies and other products normally decrease in cost the longer they are on the market due to demand decreases and production efficiency increases. At this point in the production timeline, prices are too high, and consumers are not yet impressed by the current cost-benefit ratio associated with acquiring certain products. But we are merely at the tip of the iceberg with smart appliances. Kurt Jovias, Samsung Electronics America's vice president of marketing for home appliances, suggested these initial steps are just previews of more to come. According to Jovais, while the one-way direction of communication between the consumer and product exists today, the future holds multidirectional and cross-functional interactions occurring between consumers and their products, and between products themselves.[174] These statements provoke many questions regarding future capabilities of smart appliances. Can machines take artificial intelligence a step further by monitoring our daily habits? Turning on the coffee pot when the shower is turned on in the morning? Dropping the temperature on the thermostat when all lights in the bedroom are turned off at night? Understanding and implementing the proper technologies can improve efficiency and preserve consumer loyalty as individuals grow accustomed to smart appliance producers. The market exists, leaving room for more innovation.

Google is one of the many companies out there looking to capitalize upon robotics market and innovation, specifically in driverless technology. Remember the dreaded parallel parking portion of the driving test? Many consumers know of the cars currently on the market that can now squeeze themselves into those small curbs-side spots. Google intends to venture further into that field; mass produced robotic cars with driverless capability are on the horizon. Google has already made a push in the development process, and the concept does not seem as far-fetched as it once did. The project began in 2005 when Sebastian Thrun, director of the Stanford Artificial Intelligence Laboratory and Google engineer, created the Stanley robot car with a team of Stanford students and faculty.[175] The project has since expanded and been taken under Google's wing. In the industry sector aimed at private car use, the technology has remained in the developmental stage with few driverless cars on the road, but the automotive industry has caught on to the concept. BMW and Audi provided a glimpse of the future with their driverless car in the 2014 International Consumer Electronics show.[176] The prototypes looked much like the other aesthetically pleasing cars created for commercial development, but the companies indicate commercial driverless cars will not hit the roads for another seven to ten years.[177]

These changes could rock the transportation and supply chain industry to its core, altering the landscape of transport and the movement of goods and persons. One such example of industrial change exists in Australia. An Australian mine has experienced the gains from autonomous driving robots. In a 2012 Forbes article, Tim Worstall discusses the Rio Tinto Mining Company, which operates in the Outback of the country, 60 km away from the nearest town. The mine has adopted driverless trucks, saving them a driver workforce that usually makes between $100,000 and $150,000 a year to come in and work two weeks of every month.[178] What does the additional application of this technology mean for the trucking industry? Artificial intelligence in commercial trucks will need to respond to additional stimuli not encountered by their counterparts in the isolated Rio Tinto mine, but future technology could bridge this gap, meaning structural changes to the industry. Robotics is transforming all modes of transportation, the private sector, the commercial sector, and potentially the service sector as well. In 2013 Google Ventures infused the company Uber with $250 million.[179] Uber is a company with a mobile app connecting users with drivers, with all transactions taking place on the secure internet network. The young company has expanded since its birth in 2009 to do business in over 70 cities and includes premium services with luxury brands, SUVs, hybrids, and regular taxis in its service.[180] The partnership provides a glimpse into the future; one perhaps filled with premium driverless taxi services, which can heed a consumer's request at the touch of a button. The future of transportation and service will be an interesting one to watch. We may get into vehicles and merely have to direct the vehicle's interface on where to go. What will become of the quirky cab driver-passenger conversations?

Google has remained a vanguard on the cutting edge of technological innovation. In December of 2013, the company announced its acquisition of Boston Dynamics, an engineering company known for its work on robot dogs, machines that can walk on four legs with a balance and endurance previously unseen in the field of robotics.[181] The company has worked on robotics for the military and recently released a video of its new robot named Cheetah, which was shown running on a treadmill at 29 miles per hour, a pace faster than world record holder and Olympic champion Usain Bolt.[182] The purchase of the company was the eighth robotics acquisition Google had in the last six months of 2013 alone, signaling it has a keen interest in more than just one aspect of the field. Google is not alone; other large companies, such as Amazon, are expressing interest in the future of robotics as well.

Amazon has embarked on a campaign to deliver purchases by robotic drones. Imagine having the product you ordered on Amazon placed at your feet less than 30 minutes after confirming your order. In late 2013 the company tested the advanced delivery system, but the concept is far from the implementation phase. What does this new transportation mode mean for Amazon's traditional partners, UPS and FedEx? How will the Federal Aviation Administration (FAA) monitor these new robots? The two major transport companies look forward to the application of robots as well. FedEx founder Fred Smith voiced his interest in starting drone implementation in a 2009 Wired magazine issue, listing FAA's restrictions as a source of delay.[183] Drones present an entirely new segment of product transportation, and the FAA understands this as it has plans to address the new commercial use of drones within its charters by 2015.[184]

The airborne revolution may extend past drones to encompass passenger-size jets as well. According to a 2012 article in The Economist, commercial planes are already capable of taking off, flying to a destination, and making a landing using on board computer controls.[185] These are technologies many individuals already knew were possible, but can and will planes effectively carry passengers and payloads without anyone in the cockpit? According to Lambert Dopping-Hepenstal, the director of the Autonomous Systems Technology Related Airborne Evaluation and Assessment (ASTRAEA), it is certainly feasible to have one grounded pilot looking after one or more semi-autonomous planes.[186] On board sensors, such as transponders, cameras, and infrared sensors, could warn of other planes in close proximity and help locate an unpopulated area to land in case of emergency; many of these functions are already being used with pilots in the cockpit. At the very least, future flights will have just one pilot. On-board computers have already taken upon the responsibilities of the radio operator, flight engineer, and navigator; earlier plane crews of five were not uncommon, and now the average is down to two.[187] To save on costs, airlines may alleviate one of the co-pilots of in-air duties as well. While complete autonomy is a possibility for land bound cars in the near future, the possibility of autonomous passenger airplanes is not likely. Though advancements in robotics have lessened the cost of long-range travel, it has also improved the efficacy of a more sedentary form of life.

As the world population grows and farmers reinvent productivity with mechanization, robotics will affect food production and the agricultural industry. On many mechanized farms, such as the Mulligan farm in New York detailed in a PBS report, farmers are increasing crop yield with the help of revolutionary equipment. Roaming the 1,400 acre farm, self-driving tractors analyze soil nutrition and plant more seeds in richer soil and fewer in less nutritious land.[188] However, these large advanced machines are only the beginning. Carl Dillon, a University of Kentucky professor in farm management, believes the smaller automated models are the new trend of the future; these small robots will scour the fields, applying pesticides, maintaining plants, and testing soil nutrition.[189] Farming's future will look much like its past, shifting from large roving machinery to segmented lands under the care of diligent caretakers. Working more efficiently than any human could, these new robotic workers will transform the industry. The new innovation will ultimately drive efficiency increases among small scale farmers = unable to invest the capital required to purchase the big machines most industrial farms have. These new expenditures on the technology will be not be easy to accommodate for most farms, but the benefit is the ability to rollout technology on all of the farmland in increments, thus slowly increasing crop yield and providing additional capital to purchase more machinery. The benefits will push farmers to look toward the future, employing futuristic gadgets to do one of humankind's oldest jobs: farming.

Humankind has also shaped the art of war over its long history, and the evolution appears poised to continue with robotics playing an increasing role. The U.S. military and forces around the world have updated their ranks to tackle newly emerging threats as they appear. In two recent wars fought by the U.S., military drones could be spotted in the skies of Afghanistan, and robots could be seen on the streets of Baghdad disposing of bombs and improvised explosive devices, while military men sat far off in a safe distance operating the nimble machines. These robots will be joined by more machines according to U.S. Army General Robert Cone who spoke at the Army Aviation Symposium in January of 2014. Cone, who is also head of the U.S. Army training and Doctrine Command that strategizes the Army's future, states the Army's goal is to become "a smaller, more lethal, deployable and agile force."[190] Cone's goal is to reduce manpower without suffering a corresponding reduction in firepower; in line with this, he says up to 25% of the 4,000-man force that comprises the Brigade Combat Team could be replaced with robotics by 2030.[191] The transformation would reduce military expenditures, cutting down healthcare and benefits for current and retired soldiers, and reducing the cost of the 2012 proposed budget by 25%.[192] What will the increase in mechanization mean for the military and the future of war? Society has already seen the impact of robots on war as politicians talk less about invasions and more about surgical precision strikes. The robots will not only protect the nation from outside threats, but may also protect citizens from themselves. Drones can join the cameras as technologies that monitor traffic patterns and the actions of drivers on the road, thereby freeing the police force for emergency responses and other duties. There will not be a fully automated military force or police force in the near future, but the mechanized portions will continue to grow.

BIOTECHNOLOGY

Source for both images: Luigi Guarino

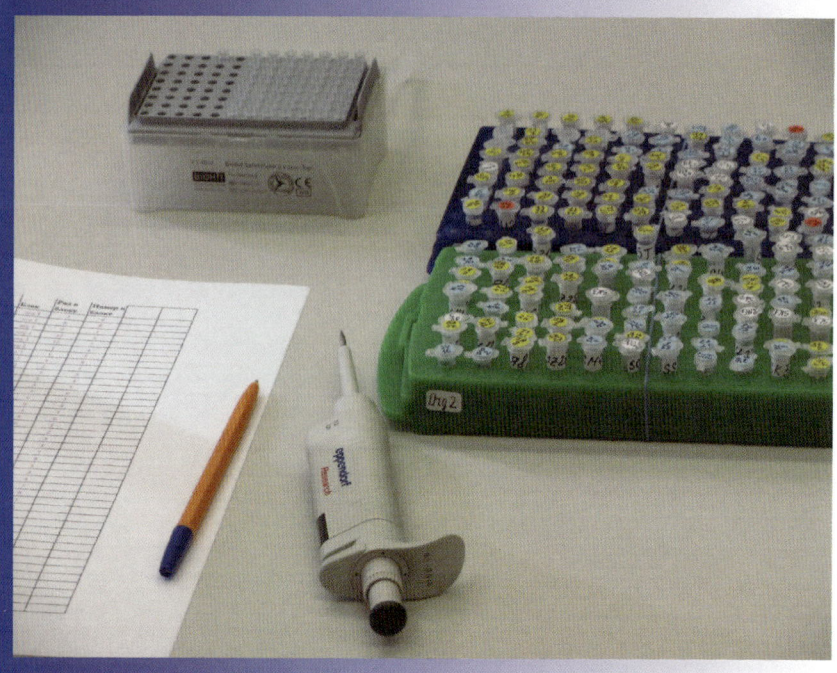

Note: Chapter originally published in Industrial Management

CHAPTER TEN

By Fariborz Ghadar & Hortense Fong

In February 2013, the U.S. Food and Drug Administration approved, for the first time, a bionic eye. The eye allows individuals with a blindness called retinitis pigmentosa to detect light and dark.[193] Then, in August 2013, two scientists, Rajesh Rao and Andrea Stocco, achieved non-invasive human brain-to-brain interfacing. Rao successfully controlled the hand movements of Stocco, who was all the way across the University of Washington's campus, with a brain signal transmitted via the Internet.[194] In September 2013, Oregon Health & Science University reported the discovery of an AIDS vaccine candidate that appears to completely clear an AIDS-causing virus from the body.[195] Everyday, mind-boggling breakthroughs are made in the realm of biotechnology. Biotechnology leverages the cell's manufacturing capabilities to put biological molecules, such as DNA and proteins, to use.

The primary areas of application of biotech are health care, food and agriculture, and industry and environment. Ernst & Young estimated the worldwide biotech industry revenue for publicly-held companies to be $89.8 billion in 2012. Of that, the U.S. accounted for $63.7 billion of the revenue.[196] While most biotech developments still occur in the United States, more and more countries are investing in biotech, and the field will soon become global. This year, Scientific American analyzed the biotech industry of 54 countries, 18 more countries than it took into consideration in 2009.[197]

Because we now live in an era of biotechnology, companies will be made and destroyed with groundbreaking inventions. The trillion dollar question is: where is biotechnology headed?

HEALTH CARE

To answer this question, we should begin by analyzing where the technology is now. Currently, the pharmaceutical industry is perhaps the biggest beneficiary of biotech. When we look at the stock performances of companies that use biotech, the strongest performers are pharmaceutical companies, such as Gilead, Aegerion Pharmaceuticals Inc., and MannKind Corp.[198] Due to aging populations in developed countries and increased wealth and access to drugs in developing countries, global drug sales hit the $1 trillion mark this year — the first time in history. Genetically engineered drugs — drugs generated with living cells rather than with chemicals — account for an estimated 10 percent of the total global prescription drugs market.[199]

Thus far, genetically-engineered drugs target diseases such as various cancers, Alzheimer's, diabetes, multiple sclerosis, heart disease, AIDS, and arthritis. Additionally, 650 new biotech drugs and vaccines for over 100 diseases are under development.[200] Large pharmaceutical companies, such as Pfizer and Merck, are investing in biosimilars, generic impersonations of biotech drugs, because of their profitability and the high sales growth of such drugs.[201] Consumers benefit from this trend because they receive access to more drug choices and prices.

FOOD & AGRICULTURE

Agribio, or agricultural biotechnology, companies have benefited from biotechnology the longest. Commercialization of biotech crops began in 1996, and, as of 2012, genetically modified (GM) seeds are planted in 28

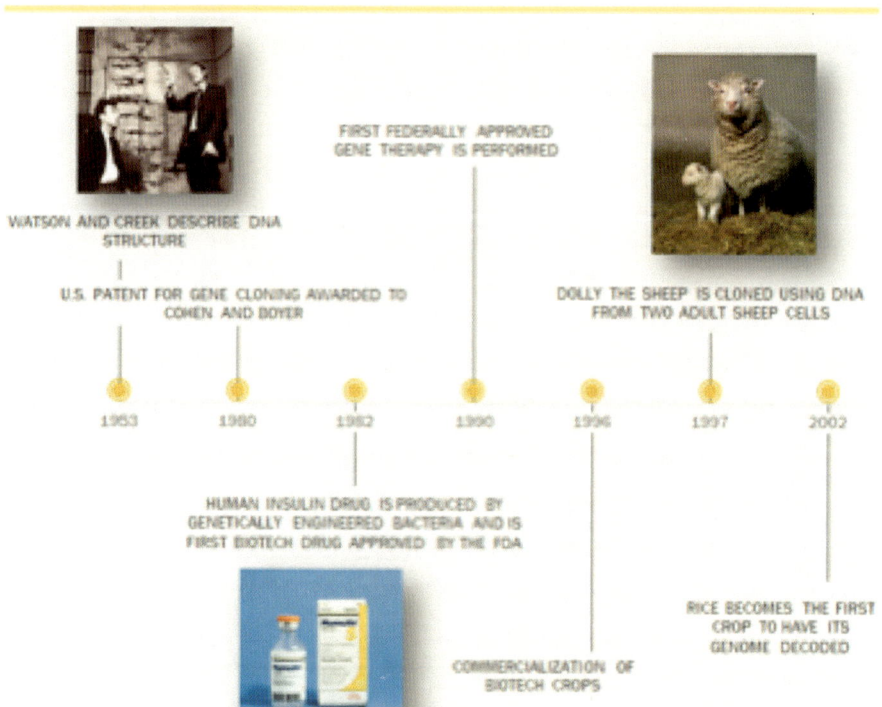

Biotechnology Advances

countries — 20 developing countries and eight industrial countries. In 2012, the U.S., Brazil, Argentina, Canada, and India grew the most biotech crops.[202] In contrast, the European Union continues to fight the use of GM crops through stringent regulations. Critics are concerned about the health and environmental effects of the crops as well as the concentration of supplying power by just a few corporations. In July 2013, Monsanto gave up trying to grow new GM crops in Europe altogether.[203] China has also faced major public opposition to GMOs.

The opposition of GM crops in Europe and China, however, is more than offset by the growth of GMOs in many developing countries. According to the International Service for the Acquisition of Agri-Biotech Applications, "for the first time in 2012, developing countries planted more hectares than industrial countries."[204] This trend is likely to continue because the benefits of biotech crops strongly appeal to developing countries. Biotech crops require less land to grow, are often resistant to disease and drought, and frequently reduce pesticide use and CO_2 emissions. Consequently, over 90 percent of the 17.3 million farmers who grew biotech crops in 2012 were small resource-poor farmers in developing countries.[205] The global market value of biotech crops in 2012 was

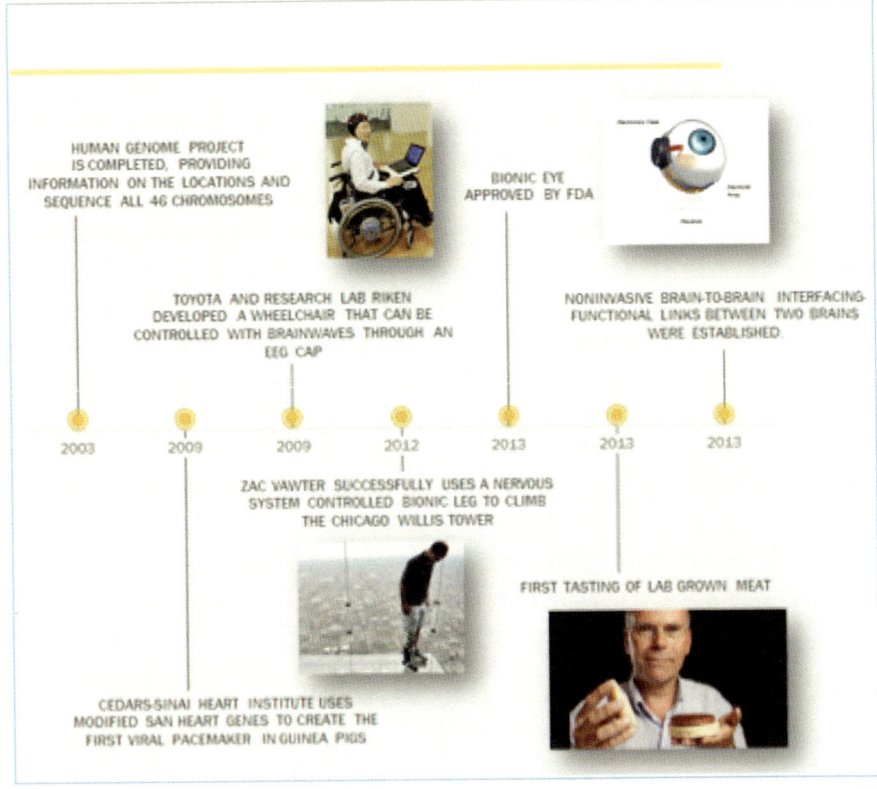

just short of $15 billion.[206] Plans to introduce biotech crops to various Asian and African countries are already in the pipeline.

Besides crops, scientists are also altering the genetic sequences of animals. A genetically engineered salmon that grows twice as fast as regular salmon is in the FDA approval process.[207] Scientists have also genetically engineered pigs, goats, and cattle for various purposes. For example, the Enviropig better digests and processes phosphorous, making it more environmentally friendly.[208]

INDUSTRY & ENVIRONMENT

Industrial and environmental biotech are the newest applications of biotechnology. Industrial biotech aims to create more sustainable manufacturing processes. For example, "green plastics" do not use petroleum in their production and instead use renewable crops. Compared to traditional manufacturing methods, industrial biotech methods produce a lower carbon footprint, create less waste, and increase yields, resulting in lower costs. Since the turn of the century, the U.S. and the E.U. have invested billions in bio-based industrial research.[209] In 2011, DuPont acquired global enzyme leader Danisco for $6.3 billion, making DuPont a leader in industrial biotechnology.[210]

For decades, petrochemical companies, such as BP, Shell, DuPont, and ExxonMobil, have invested heavily in synthetic bio research to try to develop a renewable fuel source. ExxonMobil plans to invest over $300 million in Synthetic Genomics Inc. in hopes of developing an algal-based biofuel.[211]

Going hand in hand with industrial biotech, environmental biotech aims to clean up existing waste. An example of such technology is the use of fungus in cleaning up toxic metals from water polluted by coal mines.[212]

25 Years Down the Road

Biotechnology, a global tectonic, is shifting the foundations of health care, agriculture, business, and government. The discoveries made in the field could solve many global food, health, and environmental problems, thus corporations and governments would be wise to keep their eyes and ears open to the developments in the field. Who will be the main biotechnology players 15, 20, 25 years from now?

HEALTH CARE

First, health care companies, particularly pharmaceutical companies, will continue to prosper as the global population ages and developing nations grow wealthier. According to the United Nations Population Fund, the older population "is growing at a faster rate than the total population in almost all regions of the world."[213] An aging population means more drug purchases. Furthermore, market research firm Evaluate Pharma projects that, in 2014, 50 of the top 100 drugs will have been genetically engineered.[214] As regulation and regulatory agencies catch up to the technological advancements, an unprecedented number of drugs and medical devices will be approved.

The real boom in biotech pharmaceuticals in the coming decades will occur in developing countries. The drug markets in developing countries are growing tremendously because of increased wealth and access to medicine, and shifting disease patterns. China's pharmaceutical market, worth $108 billion in 2005, is estimated to grow to $900 billion by 2020.[215] Additionally, the lower costs needed to produce a drug in developing countries make them an attractive investment.

In 25 years, we will likely be living in an era of personalized medicine. With the completion of the Human Genome Project in 2003, the decreased cost of personal genetic studies, and an ever-growing genetic database, we are closer to an era of health care tailored to one's genetic make-up. Already, biotech has developed drugs for rare diseases previously thought incurable. Through personalized medicine, patients will receive the benefits of pharmacogenomics — the personalization of drugs through the matching of specific gene variations with responses to specific medications — and of gene therapy — the replacement of disease-causing genetic mutations with healthy genes.

If we focus less on the bio and more on the tech, we enter into a more futuristic realm. Though we still do not know why we age, we have ironically discovered technologies that may allow man to live forever. Consider the following facts: On May 8, 2013, George Laskowsky, chief technical officer of Thinker Thing, a Chilean tech start-up, created the first ever real object with his mind.[216] With an electroencephalography (EEG) headset on, Laskowsky was given shapes to choose from and, based on his levels of boredom or excitement picked up by the headset, the arm of a mythical creature was designed and then built by a 3D printer.[217] Now, recall the human brain-to-brain interface between Rao and Stocco, during which a brain wave was sent across the Internet. Who's to say that we will not be able to one day record all of the decisions a person would make in varying situations, download them onto a hard drive, and then upload the data to a robot?

Consequently, human-machine interface (HMI) will be the next big area of biotech research and application. Already, we have the technology to control wheelchairs and cars with our minds. In 2009, Toyota and research lab RIKEN developed a wheelchair that can be controlled with brainwaves through an EEG cap. This idea was brought one step further with thought-controlled cars. Finally, bionic limbs are growing more and more advanced. By splicing a prosthetic to the wearer's residual nerves in the partial limb, scientists have been able to create a sense of "touch."[218]

3D printing will also contribute greatly to the area of prosthetics. Researchers at Princeton have already built a bionic ear by feeding a 3D printer with biological and nanoelectronic inks. What is even more incredible is that the bionic ear can detect frequencies a million times higher than a normal ear can. In 25 years, 3D printing will have solved the geometric complexities tissue engineers face today. Researchers will be able to create organs with blood vessels, such as livers, kidneys, and hearts.[219]

FOOD & AGRICULTURE

Despite Europe and China's current opposition, GMOs will continue to be grown, consumed as food, and used in industry. China's citizens will likely come around as they learn more about GM crops and realize the large presence of GM foods in U.S. diets.

In 2010, the U.N.'s Food and Agriculture Organization predicted that global agricultural output must increase 70 percent by 2050 to feed the world's anticipated population of 9 billion.[220] GMOs are one solution to the impending food problem. The fact that over 90 percent of GMO farmers are small resource-poor farmers in developing countries indicates a growing dependence on GM seeds. Many farmers rely on the drought-resistant, pest-resistant attributes of GM crops to feed their families and their country. Because of this growing dependence, governments will likely create regulations to prevent crop misuse and the corporate exploitation of farmers.

To increase the use of GM crops, GMO companies must prove to consumers that their products are safe to consume and are not environmentally hazardous. The GMO industry may turn to golden rice, which expresses vitamin A, to prove the benefits of biotech. While most genetically engineered crops are designed to benefit farmers, golden rice was designed to benefit consumers. The scientists who created golden rice, Ingo Potrykus and Peter Beyer, licensed their patent rights to Syngenta under the condition that the technology would be given to poor farmers in the developing world for free.[221] In 25 years, biofortified foods — foods nutritionally enhanced through genetic modification — will exist in diets throughout the world, decreasing nutrition-related diseases. We will also have foods that act as vaccines for diseases like hepatitis B and cholera; in fact, such a banana already exists.[222] One of the main concerns of GMOs is their impact on biodiversity and while some plants will go extinct as a result, new species will also develop.

With the tasting of the first piece of lab grown meat in August 2013, the market of scientifically produced meats has opened up to consideration. We will see genetically engineered animal products in supermarkets in the decades to come. Thus far, no substantial scientific or legal arguments have been made against the genetically modified salmon seeking FDA approval.[223]

INDUSTRY & ENVIRONMENT

Finally, industrial and environmental biotech companies will continue to snowball and grow. In 25 years, our manufacturing processes will be cleaner and cheaper than they are today. With 3D printers and nano-capabilities that let us build things from individual atoms and molecules, we will be able to build essentially anything we can imagine. Consultants at Smithers Rapra, the global leader in rubber, plastics, polymer, and composites testing and consulting services, believe the global industrial biotechnology market will grow at around 20 percent a year between now and 2020.[224]

Since the use of synthetic bio in industrial processes will result in a smaller carbon footprint, less industrial waste, and higher yields, urban areas in developing countries will likely invest heavily in this technology.

Rapid industrialization has led to water and air pollution and rapidly growing urban populations place a strain on infrastructure. The countries that succeed in developing robotics and clean manufacturing will be the world's future manufacturers.

PERFECT CLUSTER CONDITIONS

Genomic medicine is projected to generate $350 billion worth of economic activity and millions of jobs.[225] The advancements made in bioIT, 3D printing, nanotechnology, and robotics can be applied to biotechnology, creating the perfect recipe for a world-changing biotech cluster. Not only will the cluster create many life savings drugs and medical products, but it will also bring capital and jobs to the country that hosts it. The window of opportunity for hosting will only be open for so long, and the nation that controls the cluster will gain a significant head start in the field of biotechnology.[226]

It is uncertain why clusters form where they do, but there are two steps a country can take to increase the likelihood of building a biotech cluster. The first is to build a genomic database because genomic medicine is highly data driven. The database should include information in areas such as disease outbreaks, family history, and environmental exposures. Plunkett Research predicts that advances in systems biology — the use of molecular diagnostics, advanced computers, and genetic databases — may lead to faster and cheaper drug development. Researchers now use genetic databases of virus sequences to try to predict which virus will cause the next epidemic.[227]

The second step a country can take to kick start a cluster's development is to offer a cluster-conducive environment through legislation and capital. For example, government can offer tax incentives and can build labs with equipment that would normally cost too much for a small firm to buy. Brazil, Singapore, China, and India have invested heavily in biotechnology. China, for example, has built about ten large science parks and many smaller ones, as well as provided tax benefits and grants. The government has also invested in young biotech companies and subsidized the costs of facilities.[228] Brazil plans to reduce R&D bureaucratic restrictions and incentivize academic and industrial collaboration.[229]

Besides government, companies can support cluster growth by working with other companies. Pfizer has shared software for biotech drug research with some of its competitors, such as GlaxoSmithKline and Roche, in an effort to overcome technical obstacles. Pharmaceutical companies recognize the scientific benefits of information sharing.[230]

CATCHING UP TO THE SPEED OF INNOVATION

Every so often, we read headlines, such as "Researchers grow human brains in a lab"[231] and "Hello mothers, hello father," that leave us curious and terrified. The first article is about the use of stem cells to grow brains for research purposes. The second is about the combination of DNA from two women and one man to create a baby free of mitochondrial diseases. Biotech is a field filled with controversial subjects, and our typical response is to fight against ideas we find unnatural. Biotech, however, has been used for centuries in making wine, beer, and cheese, and in crossbreeding plants. The invention of the microscope gave us increased understanding of the cell and sped up the process of innovation. But regulation has not caught up with the speed of invention nor has society in terms of the health, legal, moral, and religious ramifications. We do not yet know the long-term effects biotech will have on our health and the environment. Issues related to privacy and insurance practices are bound to arise.

However, biotechnology holds great promise in mitigating a number of global problems, such as disease, pollution, and hunger, if implemented properly and with appropriate risk management. To develop public trust in GMOs, governments will likely implement regulations to control misuse and corporations must develop transparency protocols. Biotechnology will transform our lives over the next 25 years. To guide its development, biotech companies will work together and governments will support biotechnology's growth.

NANO-TECHNOLOGY

Source: University College London Faculty of Mathematical & Physical Sciences

Note: Chapter originally published in Industrial Management

CHAPTER ELEVEN

By Fariborz Ghadar & Kathleen Loughran

While the future effects of information technology have become easier to chart and biotechnology has developed from its nascent research beginnings into incredible commercial applications and social benefits, the ramifications of the third technological global tectonic remain more difficult to predict. This next force, nanotechnology, however, is positioned to have major global tectonic effects — yet, ironically, what it makes use of is so small that it cannot be seen with the human eye. One nanometer is one-billionth of a meter. Put another way, there are 1 million nanometers in 1 millimeter. For perspective, the width of a human hair is approximately 80,000 nanometers.[232] Nanotechnology is used to rearrange molecules so that essentially every atom can be put in its most efficient place. Ralph Merkle, Ph.D., of the Georgia Institute of Technology explains it this way: "Manufactured products are made from atoms and the properties of those products depend on how those atoms are arranged. If we rearrange the atoms in coal, we can make diamond. If we rearrange the atoms in sand and add a few other trace elements, we can make computer chips. If we rearrange the atoms in dirt, water and air, we can make potatoes."[233]

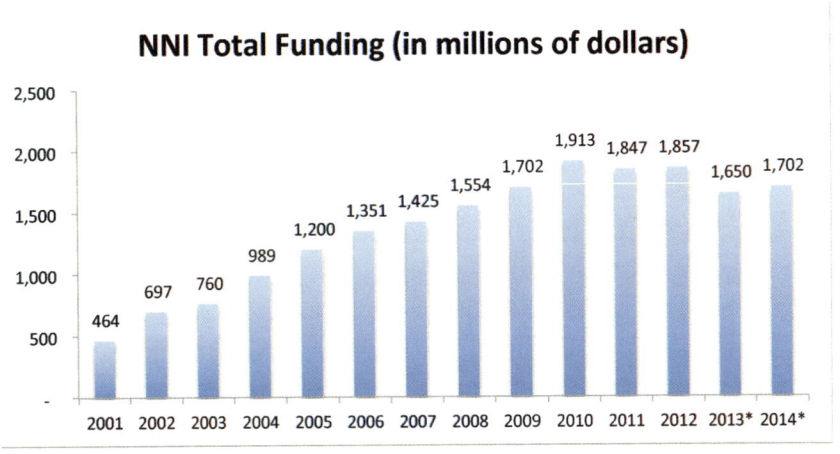

Sources: https://www.fas.org/sgp/crs/misc/RL34401.pdf; http://www.nano.gov/about-nni/what/funding

But nanotechnology is not just the miniaturization of products and rearranging of atoms. When moving from the micro level (1 micrometer is one-millionth of a meter) to the nanon level, materials exhibit new products.[234] For example, "large" particles of titanium (on the micron scale) absorb sunlight and are therefore used in some sunscreens. Unfortunately, these large particles show up white on lifeguards' noses. The nanoscale titanium particles absorb exponentially more light due to greater surface area. As a result, they appear translucent, leaving lifeguards with more natural-looking noses. Nanotech sun block is also longer lasting on the skin.[235] In addition to a larger surface area, "nanoparticles in the three-to-five nanometer range behave a lot like gas particles," said Peter Dobson, a professor of engineering science at Oxford and the founder of several nanotechnology startups.[236] Nano-enhanced materials offer new combinations of material characteristics. Scientists can use nanotechnology to produce materials that are both hard and tough, whereas hard materials are usually brittle and tough materials usually soft. And these are just some of the many different characteristics and possibilities nanotechnology presents.

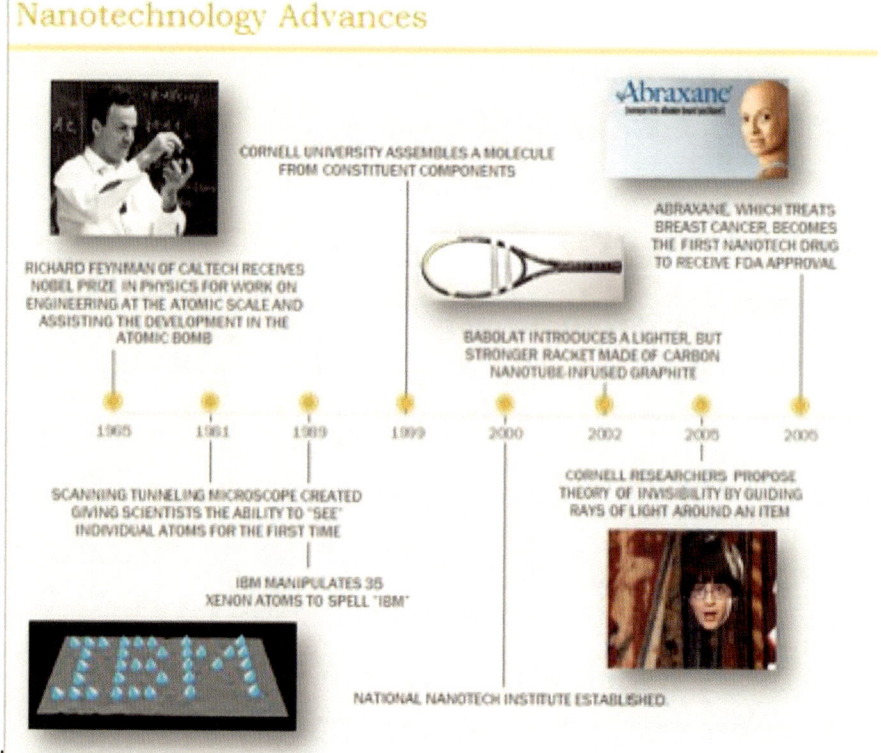

Nanotechnology Advances

Though Richard Feynman, who received the Nobel Prize in Physics in 1965, conceptualized the idea behind nanotechnology over half a century ago, we are only beginning to see the wide uses to which these emerging nanotechnologies can be put. One recent book by Jack Uldrich and Deb Newberry puts it this way: "This is not to say that nanotechnology is a far-off, fuzzy, futuristic technology. It is not. It has already established a beachhead in the economy. The clothing industry is starting to feel the effects of nanotech. Eddie Bauer, for example, is currently using embedded nanoparticles to create stain-repellent khakis. This seemingly simple innovation will impact not only khaki-wearers, but dry cleaners, who will find their business declining; detergent makers, who will find less of their product moving off the shelf; and stain-removal makers, who will experience a sharp decrease in customers. This modest, fairly low-tech application of nanotechnology is just the small tip of a vast iceberg — an iceberg that threatens to sink even the 'unsinkable' companies."[237]

Within the past decade, advancements in new instruments and technologies that provide scientists and researchers with the ability to better examine and manipulate matter now allow for a foreseeable future nan-

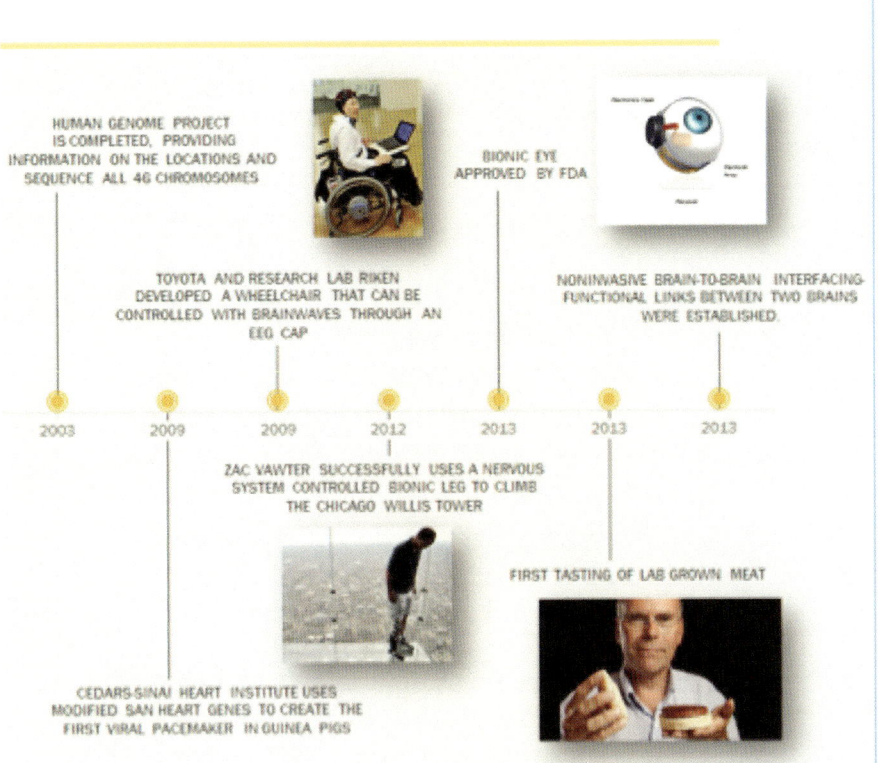

otechnology revolution. Since nanotechnology's beginnings, companies, universities, and governments around the world have invested billions in nanotech research. According to Roco et al in Nanotechnology Research Directions for Societal Needs in 2020, "Between 1990 and 2008, 17,600 companies from 87 countries were involved in nanotechnology publications and patent applications." Further, in 2009, there were $254 billion worth of products using nanotechnology in the market.[239] Though the nanotechnology industry started solely with large corporations and countries investing, that landscape is changing. According to Georgia Institute of Technology research Jan Youtie, small companies are now beginning to jump on board: "A lot of small companies are involved in novel nanomaterial development. Large companies often focus on integrating those nanomaterials into existing products or processes."[240] Thanks to the investment on the part of small and large companies, global nanotech industry output is predicted to reach $2.4 trillion as early as 2015.[241] Its future impact beyond 2015, however, is incredibly challenging to forecast, for nanotechnology has the potential to affect and to fundamentally change multiple industries.[242] Many even speculate it will usher "in the next technologically-driven Industrial Revolution."[243]

Patenting activity has also risen. In fact, the US patent office published a record number of more than 4,000 patents in 2012, which is an increase of over 2,000 patents from just three years before. Unfortunately, though, this "patent feeding frenzy" may have detrimental effects on the industry at large.[244] According to the article "Nanotech patent jungle set to become denser in 2013," "Hyperactive nanotechnology patenting is increasing costs for innovators, slowing technological development and locking away fundamental knowledge from use."[245] As a result, some have called for reprieve on patents for publicly funded research.

Despite some of these research barriers, progress in the field is still being made. For example, new drugs and diagnostic tools have already been developed with nanotechnology. Moreover, through metamaterials, we have almost achieved invisibility. A metamaterial is an artificially-created matter that bends light around it, and to the human eye, an object covered in a metamaterial appears invisible. In June 2013, Stanford University made a breakthrough in creating invisibility through the use of optical metamaterials. Previous efforts only allowed invisibility within a limited range of optical wavelengths and, therefore, colors. A Stanford research team, however, has designed a material that can bend nearly all wavelengths of light visible to the human eye.[246] Other nanotech breakthroughs include the discovery of graphene, the best heat conducting material known to man, new cancer treatments, and energy generating shirts. Penn State researcher John Badding and his team have developed the first fiber-optic solar cell. The fibers are thinner than human hair and can produce electricity. The U.S. military has already begun to invest in the fiber, which can power small electronics for soldiers in the field.[248]

In the longer term, nanotechnology will continue to impact the world in which we live. Nanotechnology researchers and developers can be broken into two camps of thought. The scientists in one camp create the products we see in the market today, such as wrinkleless shirts and high storage computer chips. They miniaturize products and take advantage of the properties of elements at the nanoscale. The scientists in the other camp believe that we will one day be able to build things from the bottom up, atom by atom. They imagine personal desktop nanofactories that build objects from the most basic raw materials. Developments made in the first camp will certainly shake the business world. A breakthrough in the second camp would transform the business world. Perhaps one day there really will be tiny, self-propelling structures that seek out and destroy cancer cells inside the human body. Nanotech could eventually change the nature of health care — moving us from what GE had called a "see and treat" world to a "predict and prevent" world.[247] Treating the human body at the cellular level could allow doctors to develop new methods to connect a number of cellular disorders, including many types of cancer. Futuristic perhaps, nantotechology also increases the medical community's understanding of brain function. A nanostructured data storage device the size of a typical human liver cell could hold information amounting to what the entire Library of Congress can store.[249] Implanted in the human brain and equipped with appropriate interface mechanisms, this device could provide insights into brain function and artificial intelligence (AI) — the technology used to create intelligent robotic machines.

Besides commercial products and health care, nanotechnology also has the potential to affect change in industries ranging from energy and the environment, to communications and computing to more. In time, nanotechnology could change all of materials science, all of computing, and much of biology.[250] A transformation of that scope could generate serious concerns over nano-ethics. It is unlikely, though, that anything would cause the nanotechnology baton to drop. We are watching a classic technological revolution unfold. The critical question for business people is where are we in that revolution and where will be in the near future. When perfected, advanced nanotechnology, also known as "molecular manufacturing," is expected to streamline production and reduce manufacturing costs so that they do not greatly exceed the cost of the required raw materials and energy.[251] With every molecule in order, production will generate less waste and be more efficient, producing low-cost, high-quality nano-engineered products. These products, cheaper to buy and to produce, have the potential to raise living standards around the world. Nanotechnological developments could also lead to a cleaner environment. The ability to create filtration systems at a molecularly precise level would improve purification of wastewater and gas from fossil fuels. Research is being done to develop nanotechnological components that break down toxic waste or the development of catalysts that decompose pollutants. Energy experts think that nanotechnology might help to reduce transmission losses by requiring the electricity grid with superconducting cable.[252] More efficient light-emitting diodes could replace wasteful incandescent and fluorescent lighting. Engineering materials that consume large quantities of energy during the manufacturing process, such as steel, aluminum, and titanium, could be replaced by resilient nanocomposites and carbon nanotubes. Scientists also hope that advances in molecular manufacturing will develop solar power into a cost-effective energy solution. Already, nanowires are having a "dramatic impact" on the efficiency of solar energy.[253]

Without a doubt, the next two decades will see more sophisticated uses of nanotechnology and better integration. While it's hard to predict the commercial impacts of nanotechnology, consumer products, health products, chemicals, and electronics will be among the most affected. And despite many challenges, nanotechnology's eventual wide spread into materials seems inevitable. Scientists will learn how to assemble atoms with stable structures predictably and profitably, and nano-tech applications will take off. They will turn it over to engineers who will develop prototypes and expertise that can be transferred to the manufacturing foremen and the marketers. Yet, as with all new technologies, nanotechnology must be developed and implemented with proper risk assessment and regulation. Despite significant breakthroughs in nanotechnology and its much-touted potential application in biomedical and materials sciences, questions still remain in the scientific community whether nanotechnology will present unique health and environmental dangers. In fact, the U.S. Environmental Protection Agency's National Center for Environmental Research funded $4 million to 12 universities for the purpose of investigating potential health and environmental impacts of nanomaterials.[254]

The incredible diversity of nano particles complicates the data-gathering process. Essentially, anything can be made nanoscale, and all materials will not be as safe as water. Determination of safe and not safe will need to be made on the specific basis of the material and the application. Like all brand new technologies, there are potential negative repercussions that have to carefully be analyzed. At the forefront of this will of course be the insurance companies that want to make sure certain elements of nanotechnology do not become the next crisis.

Nonetheless, accidents caused by careless research and development can be avoided through the implementation of appropriate safety guidelines, in both the public and private sectors. Public education and government-sponsored discourse remain critical to the successful emergence of new nanotech applications. Such dialogue will result in improved regulation and safety enforcement, and wider public support for new products and processes utilizing the technology. Given the potential for nanotechnology to improve the manufacture, sale, and transport of goods and services, business leaders should spearhead efforts to mainstream and employ this technology as it develops. But before investors get out their checkbooks, they need to be aware that it could be years before we see the full effects of the industry and resolve many of its complications. And, as with most new technologies, the resolutions will owe much to trial and error with a good dose of luck.

CONFLICT

Source: http://www.flickr.com/photos/rafahkid/3159461534

CHAPTER TWELVE

By Fariborz Ghadar & Kathleen Loughran

Throughout history, conflict has notoriously been a shaping force that has largely influenced many governmental decisions and actions. With advancements in technology, knowledge and diplomatic relations, however, the dynamics of conflict have changed over time — and the 21st century marks another major shift in this landscape.

If we look back thousands of years, conflict was often settled through the appearance of combat between two large armies. In actuality, the strongest soldier from each army would square off, and the victor would claim triumph for his entire country. These head-to-head encounters eventually evolved into large-scale battles, but the fighting was still generally contained to a specific location, where civilians could watch on the hills. The war for America's independence changed this formula, when the Patriots ushered in new tactics to fighting, such as shooting behind trees in dense woods. Nonetheless, the conflict remained between two distinct parties. This altered with the onset of WWI and WWII, when individual countries banded together and fought the opposing side, and surrogate wars were fought in multiple places. After WWII, the potential threat of conflict became even more disconcerting, as technological advancements, such as nuclear power, gave way to the possibility of total global destruction. The Cold War and particularly the Cuban missile crisis brought fear into the hearts of many. Despite these apprehensions, conflict was still able to remain mostly manageable, thanks to the influence of large superpowers. As alluded to previously, the 21st century has fundamentally changed this paradigm. As Anne-Marie Slaughter, former director of policy planning at the U.S. State Department, said "The two wars launched in response to 9/11 — one justifiably in Afghanistan and the other unjustifiably in Iraq — are likely to be the last examples of 20th century-style warfare: large-scale multi-year conflicts involving the grand invasion of one country by another."[255] If this is the case, what then will conflict of the 21st century look like?

We've already witnessed the early stages of what conflict will increasingly become. As the international system has shifted away from a bipolar balance of power, the threat of global destruction via nuclear power has dissipated. But naturally that does not mean the threat of conflict has been dispelled. Rather, the proliferation of civil, intrastate, and non-state conflicts has gradually replaced wars of containment. In the summer of 2006, "Hezbollah clearly demonstrated the ability on non-state actors to study and deconstruct the vulnerabilities of Western style militaries, and devise appropriate countermeasures."[256] Though not all countries classify Hezbollah as a terrorist organization, it is not controlled by the Lebanese government and has participated in "numerous anti-US terrorist attacks."[257] The Hezbollah has continued to wreak havoc in Lebanon and the surrounding area. Partially because of organizations like Hezbollah, the number of intrastate conflicts is now far higher than the number of interstate conflicts, and that trend is expected to continue through 2025 and beyond.

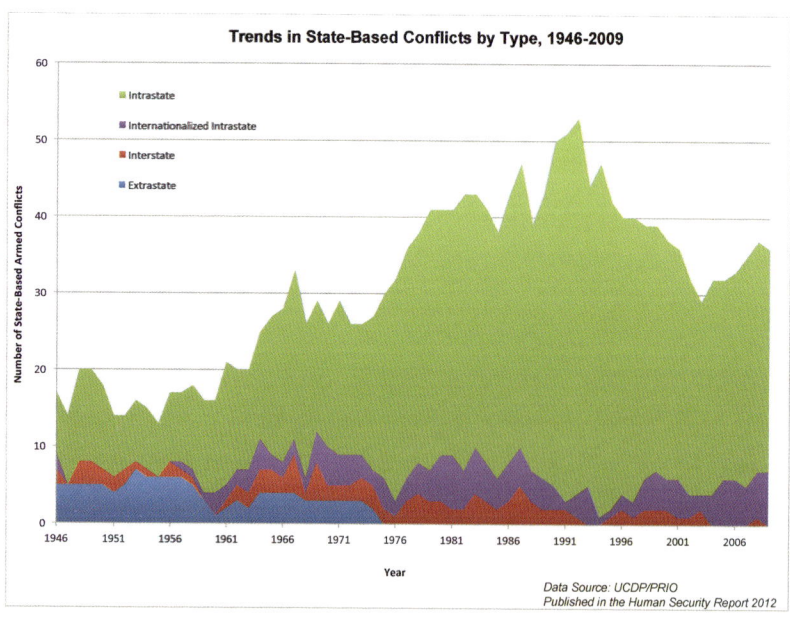

Although these types of conflict have resulted in fewer deaths on a whole, they are "often characterized by extreme brutality toward civilians."[258] While civilians only represented 5 percent of total war causalities during WWI, today they equate for a startling 75 percent.[259] Because these attacks frequently come without an exact return address, retaliation can be difficult to determine. As stated by Frank G. Hoffman of the Potomac Institute for Policy Studies, "In the past, analyzing the nature of the problem was relatively simple in that the adversaries were well defined and this provided a relative sharp focus."[260] This new style of conflict, however, has led to the retaliating force sometimes deciding to invade the area because of the ill-defined adversary, and conflict is thus taken into the local streets. Because of advancements in technology and the inability to pinpoint the return address, multiple parties have also taken to using drones to retaliate. Furthermore, because most of these conflicts occur intrastate, conflict is inherently more prevalent in civilians' lives.

The tectonic force of conflict on the global economy influences investment, creates and destroys markets, and dictates trade. Domestic, interstate, and global conflicts have historically impacted investors, managers, and multinational corporations through diverse and evolving patterns. From domestic, religious, and ethnic disputes to worldwide terrorism, conflict is a shaping force in the global economy. When aid and support from their parent superpowers disappeared, countries once important to Cold War strategy, such as Afghanistan, Guatemala, and the Democratic Republic of Congo (formerly Zaire), often succumbed to violent conflict. Internal factions and neighboring states, long suppressed by international politics, fought for power and resources. Over the past 25 years, such countries have not only become centerpieces of rising ethnic, religious, and border strife but also breeding grounds for terrorism.

Civil and intrastate conflicts continually threaten to expand to regional and international political and economic stability. The ongoing strife in Central Africa and the Middle East highlights the debilitating effect of conflict on economic development for countries involved directly in the conflict as well as for neighboring countries drawn into the hostilities. Fighting has resulted in massive cross-border refugee flows, increased levels of disease in refugee camps, and the disruption of food and medical aid to those most in need. Typically, war-torn countries record little to no economic growth, as military spending balloons and political instability dampens foreign investment and tourism.[261] In fact, according to a study conducted by Solomon W. Polachek and Daria Sevastianova, "Estimates indicate that civil war reduces annual growth by .01 to .13 percentage points, and high-intensity interstate conflict reduces annual growth by .18 to 2.77 percentage points… The detrimental effect of conflict on growth is intensified when examining non-democracies, low income countries, and countries in Africa."[262] Countries will only be able to restore civil society and re-invigorate their ailing economies if they can establish stable governments and a peaceful environment in which companies can operate. Unfortunately, this is a difficult hurdle to overcome not only because of the challenge of reaching stability itself, but also because of the numerous forces working against it. According to an OECD paper titled "Think global, act global: Confronting global factors that influence conflict and fragility," "Fragile states are attractive to transnational organised crime (TOC) as transit points due to their institutional fragmentation and opportunities to exploit social and economic inequalities with little prospect of any legal or social backlash."[264]

Although transnational and civil strife often occurs in politically and economically marginal countries, the September 11 terrorist attacks on the U.S. brought these failing states to the center of world attention. In the aftermath of 9/11, the international community realized it could no longer afford to neglect ethnic, religious, and border conflicts in peripheral states such as Afghanistan. The U.S. State Department has already developed a "States of Concern" list, declaring Sudan, Iran, Syria, North Korea, Cuba, and Libya as potential threats to international security. Furthermore, individuals have increasingly begun to operate independently of terrorist organizations in countries not typically associated with having terrorist attacks. For a more explicit example, consider the Boston Marathon bombings, which occurred on April 15, 2013 and have since been marked as the most detrimental terrorist attack since 9/11. Unlike 9/11, however, this attack wasn't spearheaded by a larger terrorist organization. Rather, two legal immigrants from Dagestan, Russia, Tamerlan and Dzhokhar Tsarnaev, are suspected of the attack that killed three people and injured nearly 300. According to an article published in The New York Times, "The portrait investigators have begun to piece together of the two brothers suspected of the Boston Marathon bombings suggests that they were motivated by extremist Islamic beliefs but were not acting with known terrorist groups — and that they may have learned to build bombs simply by logging onto the online English-language magazine of the affiliate of Al Qaeda in Yemen…"[265] Hoffman further predicts that the United States will continue to face a "broadening number of challenges… These include traditional, irregular, terrorist and disruptive threats or challengers."[266]

World business leaders cannot overlook the threat of terrorism, especially given the potential significant costs of such violence. The 9/11 attacks resulted in an estimated $105 billion in immediate damages, including loss of life, destruction of property, and short-term depression of economic activity.[267] The prolonged threat of terrorism compounds these losses. Under continued threats of violence, consumer confidence decreases, perceived investor risk and interest rates increase, fuel prices become more unpredictable, and critical industries such as airlines, restaurants, and tourist services can falter. Given the close economic ties between countries, attacks in one nation often reverberate throughout the international business system, causing regional economic depression. According to the Asia-Pacific Economic Cooperation paper, "a study of 200 countries from 1968 to 1979 showed that a doubling in the number of terrorist incidents decreased bilateral trade between targeted economies by approximately six percent." In 2002, after the Bali tragedy, Indonesia lost approximately one percent of its GDP receipts.[268] These examples only begin to illustrate the severe impact of terrorism on international business.

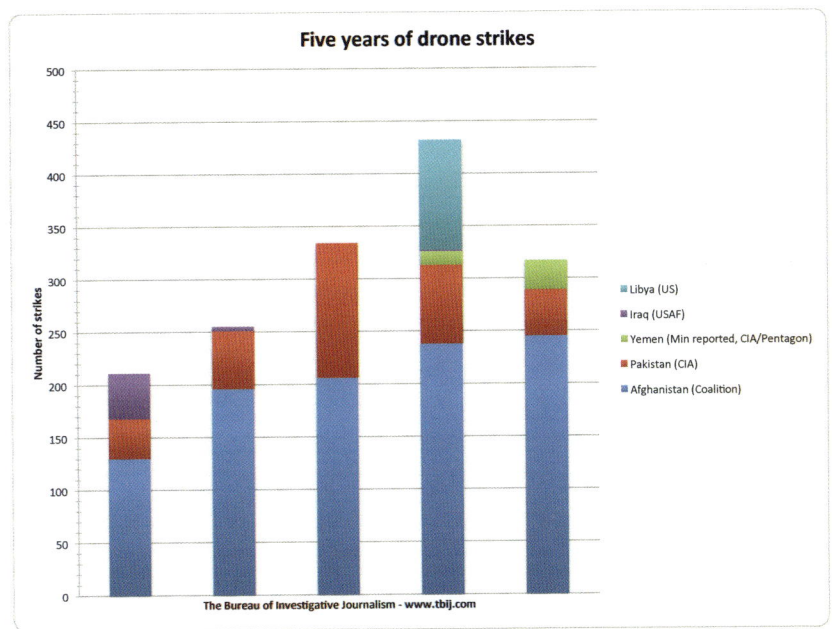

In the future, corporations will also continue to fight a war on a new form of terrorism: cyber terrorism. In August 2012, for example, 30,000 of Saudi Aramco's workstations were attacked by Shamoon Malware.[269] Fortunately these computers were not linked to the company's oil production because one can only imagine what the ramifications would be to oil prices if they had been. Though not nearly as devastating as violent conflict, cyber terrorism poses a substantial threat to any firm that relies on computer systems and/or operates online. A 2013 study by the Center for Strategic and International Studies called "The Economic Impact of Cybercrime and Cyber Espionage," concluded that the U.S. loses up to

500,000 jobs a year and as much as $100 billion each year as a result of cyber espionage.[270] Nearly every important corporation is now computer dependent, making cyber terrorism and espionage a serious current and future threat to business. With such dependence on information and networking technology, the costs of vulnerabilities to cyber terrorism in the United States and abroad could be devastating to national security and the economy.

The specter of such increased and diversified forms of conflict presents downside risks to companies and national economies. Yet these risks are more contained and at the same time require new methods and technologies that present opportunities associated with addressing these dangers. The first is that, by definition, the new dangers associated with asymmetric warfare suggest the need for greater public-private sector cooperation. To meet the challenge of defending critical infrastructure and a range of other key homeland contingencies, governments and companies will need to work together at much higher levels of cooperation and coordination. This presents a constellation of challenges and opportunities to companies that have positioned themselves as partners in addressing the risks of conflict. Second, companies working to develop technological responses to new dangers associated with conflict (sensors, vaccines, and data mining, among others) can position themselves to contribute and provide solutions from the new requirements we face. Industry can and will be expected to help and lead through the development and application of new technologies and practices, as the U.S. considers whether it wants to engage in other countries' intrastate conflicts. Regardless, the U.S. will continue to shift its spending from defense to security expenditures, as the nature of conflict continues to change. We've already witnessed the early stages, such as increased airport security and prevalence of cameras in large cities. But as people continue to be more mobile and centralized in cities, the government will be forced to consider and analyze appropriate measures for protecting its people in the changing face of conflict.

GOVERNANCE

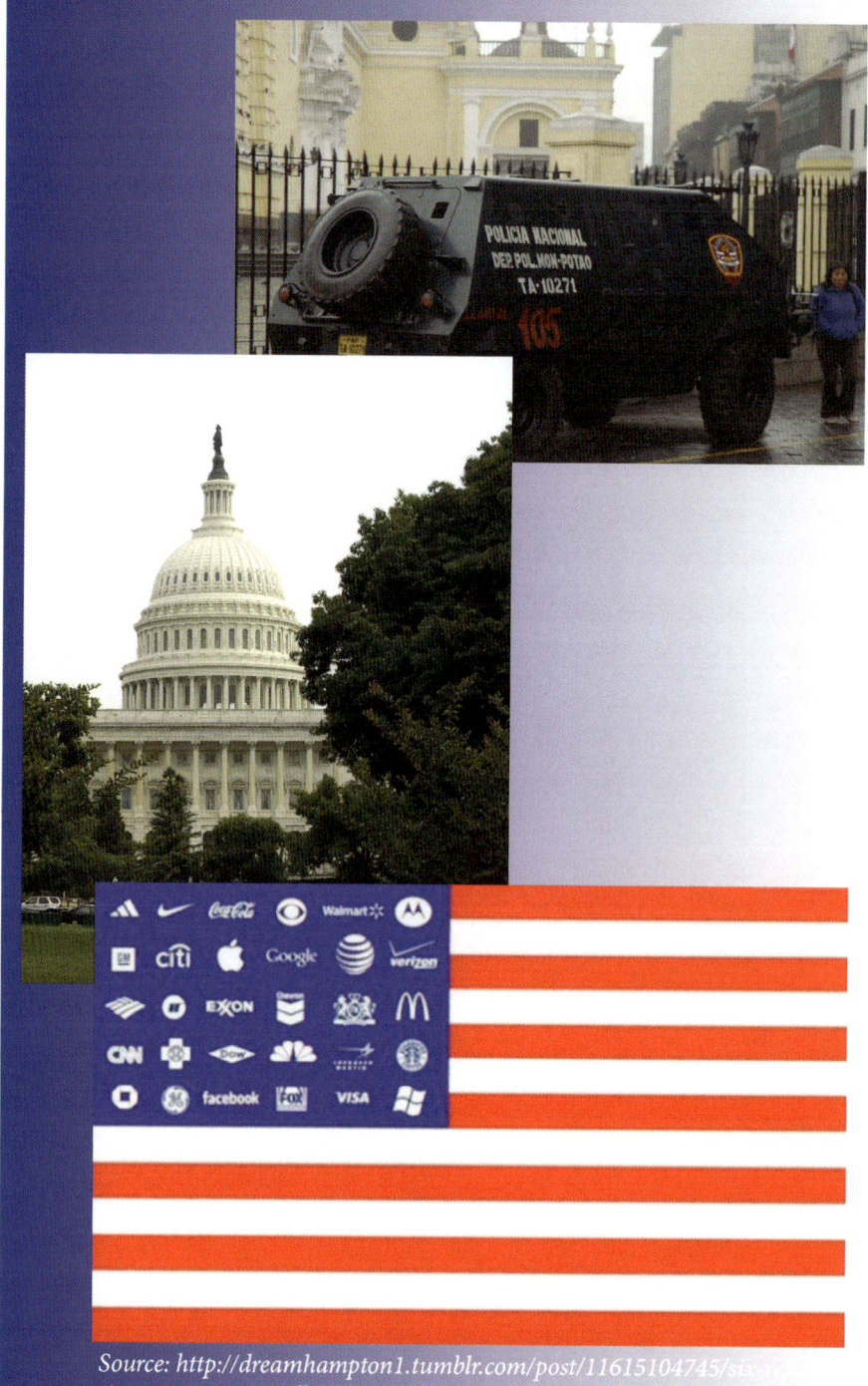

Source: http://dreamhampton1.tumblr.com/post/11615104745/six-observations-on-occupy-wall-street-click

CHAPTER THIRTEEN

By Fariborz Ghadar & Kathleen Loughran

The complexity of governance is difficult to capture in a simple definition. Obviously, the need for governance exists any time a group of people comes together to accomplish an end. By nature, governance can be messy, tentative, unpredictable, and fluid. It is further complicated by the fact that it involves multiple actors, not just a single helmsman. The actors on this stage have changed and evolved over the years, and governance has had to respond accordingly. We once all belonged to small tribal communities governed by a chieftain living among us. Those communities grew to larger nation states governed by kings who were geographically and culturally set apart from the majority of the people. Central governments developed to help navigate this process for both the principal actors and the affected audience. And, as the kings and central governments implemented hefty taxation, governance in many countries began to be shaped into democracies, allowing the public to influence tax utilization. Legislative, judicial, and executive branches of government evolved to address people's needs and wellbeing. Classic reforms changed how governments instituted law, taxation, and social welfare. In the early 1900s, however, the rise of corporations, both local and multinational companies (MNCs), modified the system of governance and the struggle for social and economic reform and progress. Corporations such as United Fruit Inc., which benefited from the global advance of democracy and capitalism, grew into large and powerful enterprises.[271] In just a few decades, multinational companies rivaled some governments as influential actors in state policy and decision making. Corporations then developed their own governance, consisting of audit, finance, compliance, and compensation committees, as well as a board of directors, to deal with government requirements.

By the mid to late 1900s, MNCs themselves had become agents of governance and targets for reform.[272] Their policies had enormous impact on the economic wellbeing of the states in which they operated, as well as the livelihoods of their vast pools of employees in countries across the world. Consider that "Of the world's 100 largest economic entities in 2009, 44 are corporations. If you look at the top 150 economic entities, the proportion of corporations rises to 59%," according to an article titled "Corporate Clout 2012: The Influence of the World's Largest 100 Economic Entities."[273] Progressively, corporations have been regarded as more than wealth-maximization entities. The presence of corporate titans in developing countries gives corporations a hand in deciding issues that have a significant economic and social impact. In many cases, this presence has benefited states and contributed to economic growth and peace. Despite being a boon for countries, the effects of multinational corporations' power have been, on occasion, a double-edged sword. While bringing jobs and economic growth to many otherwise impoverished regions of the world, multinational corporations have sometimes eroded the strength of state governments and have often been criticized for putting investor interests before those of the societies in which they operate. Corporations have been increasingly scrutinized in their environmental practices, and civil societies are demanding more transparency, corporate accountability, and responsible corporate citizenship. Today, civil society continues to press for reforms in corporate patterns — from corporate citizenship to corporate social responsibility to what P&G refers to as "corporate social opportunity."[274]

While citizens in many countries have felt disconnected from their governments and powerless against the influence of multinational corporations, a plot twist has occurred with the rapid development of a new power broker: the nongovernmental organization (NGO). As an outgrowth of democracy, the NGO has grown as a mechanism by which civil society can seek to increase its control over corporate and government decision-making. They have effectively carved themselves a niche into global civil society often targeting their actions against governments and corporations they deem detrimental. To specifically ensure companies don't engage in undesirable behaviors, many NGOs keep a watchful eye. For example, Transparency International annually publishes a Corruption Perceptions Index, Bribe Payers Index, and a Global Corruption Barometer. Among the reports is the $1.6 billion in fines that Siemens had to pay to settle bribery accusations made by American and European authorities.[275] Additionally, groups such as Consumers Union, CorpWatch, Greenpeace International, Policy Action Network, and Public Citizen have captured the support of youth and many consumer and other groups. They have leveraged the revolution in information technology to force transparency on traditionally closed companies and governments. Rapid growth since 1994, largely thanks to the rise of the Internet, their popular support, and charge of information, has made

NGOs a current and powerful addition to world governance system.

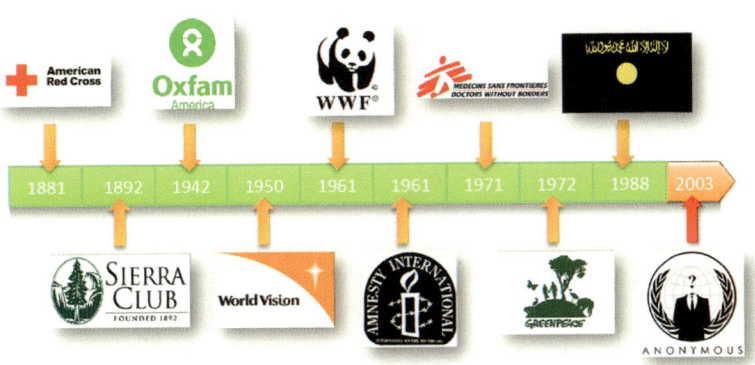

Over the next 25 years, we expect NGOs to play an increasingly important role in governance. One of the reasons they have been able to quickly garner such significant influence is their ability to use the Internet and social media as a platform for communication. While NGOs have existed for many years, their power and importance as stakeholders in governance has only increased recently with the revolution of information flow. NGO websites and Internet blogs provide alternative perspectives and news for everyone (particularly for those living in areas that lack a free press) while linking people across borders who share a common global cause.

The advent of global telecommunications allows NGOs in even the most remote countries to connect with the global media and subsequently to global politics. It has also afforded the opportunity for NGOs to more easily make their voices heard. NGOs such as Amnesty International, Doctors Without Borders, and the World Wildlife Fund spawned as a method for people to supplement and often check the power of governments and corporations. And, as the Internet continues to make it easier for such organizations to thrive, we can expect more NGOs to leverage such power. The number of NGOs holding consultative status with ECOSOC has skyrocketed from 41 in 1946 to well over 3,000 today.[276] Yet, worldwide, thousands more exist. According to the NGO website, "the number of internationally operating NGOs is around 40,000."[277] This number, however, only represents NGOs that operate in multiple countries. If we take into account the number of NGOs working in individual countries, that number would be even higher, into the millions. All of this points to the increased expression of popular sentiments through organized democratic action. The fact that corporate social responsibility initiatives are sometimes driven by governments and other times by NGOs illustrates the influence and power that NGOs have attained. For a more explicit example, consider that "the World Bank estimates that over 15 percent of total overseas development aid is channeled through NGOs."[278]

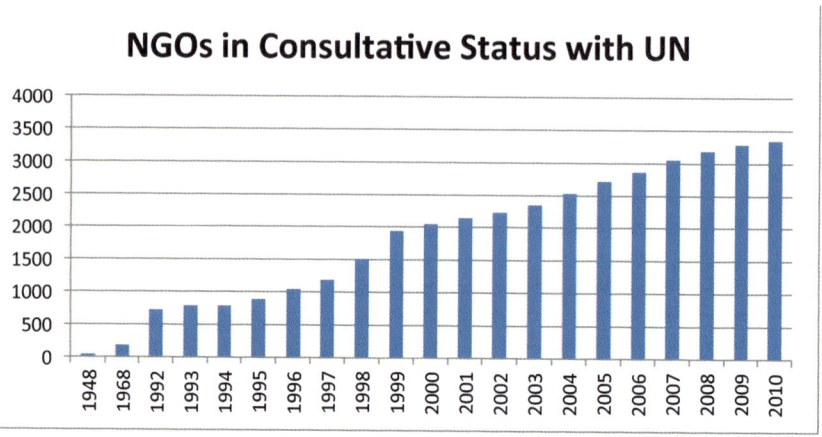

Source: http://www.globalpolicy.org/images/pdfs/NGOs_in_Consultative_Status_with_ECOSOC_by_Category.pdf

Because of the dramatic growth in the power of NGOs, they now serve an important function in governance issues. NGOs interact with both corporate and traditional state government interests. Through public education and information dissemination, NGOs are able to pressure governments and corporations to be more accountable and transparent about issues ranging from human rights to environment to labor standards. Corporations cannot afford to ignore these organizations that have the backing of a younger generation of civil society and the power to report information quickly and accurately. Unfortunately, NGOs have also risen in support of less constructive social goals. Desperate and discontent people have supported violent NGOs such as Al Qaeda to express their grievances. NGOs, their goals, and their methods bring questions relating to conflict, including terrorism and government regulation.

As they grow in power, NGOs will be required to meet international and local accountability and transparency standards. These organizations will need to maintain a balance between volunteerism and activism, and they will need to develop and maintain the professionalism necessary to operate competitively in nonprofit and business environments. Looking forward, NGOs are expected to experience a period of pronounced pressure on their own governance structures not dissimilar to what the private sector experienced in the wake of the Enron events. Looming issues such as legitimacy (Where do NGOs get their authority?) and operational characteristics (How efficiently are they operated?) will assume ever-sharper definition. As a result, in the next few decades, we can expect that NGOs will become even better organized, increasingly active as stakeholders, more media savvy, and more connected to their constituencies by Internet and telecommunication technologies.

But NGOs are not the only ones who have taken advantage of the current IT revolution. With increased access to unfiltered, uncensored communication channels enhancing mobilization abilities, the general public no longer has to rely on traditional news media.[279] In this new technologically-equipped environment, virtually anyone can become a reporter through snapping a photograph on their smart phone and posting it on the web, through blogging about current events, and through tweeting the latest news in 140 characters or fewer. This newfound ability coupled with a surge in the public distrust of traditional media has largely placed the power into the hands of the individual. As a result, individuals and small groups of people have made it a point to act as the moderator. When it comes to rallying people, the internet and social media has proven to be more effective than street protests as exemplified in Egypt in January 2011, when thousands of Egyptians marched to demand a new government — a movement that was then broadcasted worldwide by its very catalyst: social media. Bringing the protests in the streets of Egypt into global conversation, social media saw a revolution that led the Egyptian government to shut it down denying its populace access in an effort to stop protests. Events like these and Iranian Green Movement led Hillary Clinton to equate the Internet to "the public space of the 21st century — the world's town square..."[280] The scarcity of transparency has led NGOs and individuals to utilize the strength of social media to influence policy.[281] It's imperative to note, however, that social media only provides visibility not organization, especially in the hard to reach places — for that, manpower is needed.

Although WikiLeaks does not fall into any of the traditional categories of media, it is part of the changing landscape in the modern technological world. Examples from WikiLeaks range from hacking Sarah Palin's email to getting military video of an Apache helicopter shooting Iraqi civilians and journalists. Information needs to be stored somewhere, but, when it's on the internet, it means it can also be found and retrieved in one form or another. WikiLeaks scares governments, politicians, and business leaders because the internet is so open and easily hacked. The notion of "Security" and "Privacy" are illusions, yet denying breaches to security is often easier than admitting vulnerability to attacks. Despite some problems associated with WikiLeaks and NGOs, they can force leaders to be more open, creating healthier democracies and corporations. In turn, forcing businesses to strengthen their own lines of communication and to take all stakeholders into account, as well. They could also further incentivize corporations to embrace creating shared social value, be it with an NGO or independently.

As a result of WikiLeaks, Obama ended up having to revisit the Secret Courts and has been under pressure to make government actions more transparent. Additionally, Wikileaks have helped spark rebellions in oppressed countries and expose cronyism and dysfunctional governments. But WikiLeaks is not the only entity that has led to rebellions. Although much of the attention given to Anonymous has been bad press, it has been an integral part in assisting Arab Spring activists by providing essential logistics and media attention. Similarly, it assisted with the BART protests and Occupy protests in the west. In an effort to directly attack oppressors that try and limit telecommunications, Anonymous crashed the Tunisian Stock Market. Although short-lived, the fact that a small group was able to affect the global financial markets is nothing to turn a blind eye. This movement with countless actions has bred a culture quickly spreading across the world.[282] The lessons that can be learned from horizontally organized NGOs and individuals' actions is that both are here to stay. Anonymous also shows the dangers of the internet and cybersecurity for many companies due to the relative ease at which it can cause sizable damage to MNCs and individuals. For example, Anonymous has caused trouble ranging from stalling Visa and Mastercard websites to stealing the data of HBGary Federal, seizing the CEO's Twitter account, and then allegedly remotely erasing his iPad.

The interaction of these actors will give rise to three major governance trends: the spread of democracy, improved corporate governance, and the continued emergence of NGOs and of individuals as corporate and government watchdogs. These changes in governance will impact internal business processes and shape the international environment in which corporations trade and invest. To remain viable in the future, business leaders will need to adjust their corporate strategies to address these inevitable political, corporate, and civil developments. During the next few decades, advancements in governance will unfold like the domino effect; businesses will challenge governance to improve the rule of law; governments will more tightly regulate corporate operations, and NGOs and individuals will report to civil society on both business and country proceedings. Everyone will begin to cross track and monitor each other's movements. No one — from large corporations, to NGOs, to governments, to individuals — is safe from being scrutinized and analyzed, which will also essentially bring an end to privacy. As this all unfolds, these trends in governance will hopefully improve the quality, dignity, and efficiency of international business across the globe.

CONCLUDING REMARKS

Many of these Global Tectonics, by virtue of their gradual nature, will fail to capture headlines. They will never be the subjects of debate in boardrooms dominated by short-term concerns; they will be overshadowed by other day-to-day events. And many, because they will slowly and subtly unfold, will go unnoticed by governments, companies and other organizations.

The reality, however, is that each of the Global Tectonic forces will have a significant impact on the world's dynamics in the years ahead. Each will play a significant role in determining the way in which we live, the nature and rate of economic activity around us, the ways in which we interact with other people, and, ultimately, the prospects we provide for our children and grandchildren. Each carries with it simultaneous dangers and opportunities. And each tectonic will have a number of inflection points — points at which leadership decisions will mean the difference between success and failure.

Especially in light of these longer-range trends, businesses need to be "tuned in" to these geopolitical tectonic trends to stay competitive. More and more, we believe the capacity to anticipate and to adapt business operations will be an increasingly critical comparative advantage. In short, the outlook for businesses will become more contingent on their capacity to develop and to implement a strategic vision in the face of ever more onerous shorter-term pressures. That is no small task.

The record suggests this kind of innovation in long-range positioning carries with it high premiums. We believe the premiums associated with rapid innovation will be even more significant in the future, as the forces of the creative destruction continue to reward rapid adapters and remove slow or non-adapters from the picture.

There are many compelling examples of companies that have succeeded or failed as a result of their capacity to adapt to changing conditions. There will be many more. Recently, the rapid development and diffusion of technology is the obvious force that has fundamentally transformed the marketplace. Other forces, as we have argued, will follow. The winners and losers will be determined by their capacity to innovate: first, to innovate in the framework of their operations to exploit the changing business environment, and second and more importantly, to adapt their strategies to account for anticipated change.

These dynamics, we expect, will apply not only to companies, but also to governments both big and small, and to other organizations ranging from NGOs to educational institutions. The outlook for these groups will also be determined by the degree to which they can look forward to the various trends at work and to the ways in which they can recalibrate their goals and operations to reflect the world they expect to see.

Moreover, we wish to stress the complexities inherent in these broad global trends and to emphasize the need to avoid generalizations and broad-brush conclusions. For example, by dividing the world along "developed" country and "developing" country lines, with all the methodological and other ambiguities it implies, there is the danger that the complexities associated with the global tectonics — the granularities within and between these groups — will be lost. To draw from our discussion of both China and India in the Knowledge Dissemination chapter, both countries are making significant strides in education, yet they will have to contend with growing populations, potential youth bulges and urbanization issues.

The bottom line is organizations need good, effective vision that can differentiate between salient elements and the "background noise" of less important elements, which serve to clutter their capacity to navigate. They need to appreciate the granularity of the many tectonic forces around them without losing the big picture. By definition, it is a significant challenge to develop and then to maintain such effective vision, let alone ensure it is implemented operationally.

APPENDIX

SOURCES

1. United Nations Department of Economic and Social Affairs Population Division "World Population Prospects: The 2012 Revision." http://www.google.com/url?sa=t&rct=-j&q=&esrc=s&source=web&cd=8&ved=0CGQQFjAH&url=http%3A%2F%2Fesa.un.org%-2Funpd%2Fwpp%2FDocumentation%2Fpdf%2FWPP2012_%2520KEY%2520FINDINGS.pdf&ei=9shvUpbiNtOp4APA-YDwCA&usg=AFQjCNHhhCmQLvVrujVuLZDt, C6h8yrjgvA&sig2=beNS-YlbSZynNsrSfzxzXuA&bvm=bv.55123115,d.dmg (October 2013).
2. U.S. Census Bureau "International Programs." www.census.gov/ipc/www/worldpop.html (October 2013).
3. United Nations Department of Economic and Social Affairs Population Division "World Population Prospects: The 2012 Revision." http://www.google.com/url?sa=t&rct=-j&q=&esrc=s&source=web&cd=8&ved=0CGQQFjAH&url=http%3A%2F%2Fesa.un.org%-2Funpd%2Fwpp%2FDocumentation%2Fpdf%2FWPP2012_%2520KEY%2520FINDINGS.pdf&ei=9shvUpbiNtOp4APA-YDwCA&usg=AFQjCNHhhCmQLvVrujVuLZDtC6h8yrjgvA&sig2=beNS-YlbSZynNsrSfzxzXuA&bvm=bv.55123115,d.dmg (October 2013).
4. Worldmapper: The World As You've Never Seen It "Population 2300." http://www.worldmapper.org/display.php?selected=12 (October 2013).
5. Lutz, Wolfgang. "The End of Wolrd Population Growth in the 21st Century: New Challenges for Human Capital Formation and Sustainable Development." International Institute for Applied Systems Analysis. July 2004. http://www.iiasa.ac.at/Research/POP/pub/worldbook04.html (September 2004).
6. Haub, Carl. "Fact Sheet: World Population Trends 2012." Population Reference Bureau. July 2012. http://www.prb.org/Publications/Datasheets/2012/world-population-data-sheet/fact-sheet-world-population.aspx (Octover 2013).
7. Haub, Carl. "Fact Sheet: World Population Trends 2012." Population Reference Bureau. July 2012. http://www.prb.org/Publications/Datasheets/2012/world-population-data-sheet/fact-sheet-world-population.aspx (October 2013).
8. Haub, Carl. "Fact Sheet: World Population Trends 2012." Population Reference Bureau. July 2012. http://www.prb.org/Publications/Datasheets/2012/world-population-data-sheet/fact-sheet-world-population.aspx (October 2013).
9. Haub, Carl. "Fact Sheet: World Population Trends 2012." Population Reference Bureau. July 2012. http://www.prb.org/Publications/Datasheets/2012/world-population-data-sheet/fact-sheet-world-population.aspx (October 2013).
10. Haub, Carl. "Fact Sheet: World Population Trends 2012." Population Reference Bureau. July 2012. http://www.prb.org/Publications/Datasheets/2012/world-population-data-sheet/fact-sheet-world-population.aspx (October 2013).
11. Gautreaux, Sergio B. "Understanding China's Internal Migration." *International Policy Digest*, March 3, 2013. http://www.internationalpolicydigest.org/2013/03/03/understanding-chinas-internal-migration/ (October 2013).
12. United Nations Population Fund "Linking Population, Poverty and Development." http://www.unfpa.org/pds/trends.htm (October 2013).
13. Haub, Carl. "Fact Sheet: World Population Trends 2012." Population Reference Bureau. July 2012. http://www.prb.org/Publications/Datasheets/2012/world-population-data-sheet/fact-sheet-world-population.aspx (October 2013).
14. United Nations Population Fund "Linking Population, Poverty and Development." http://www.unfpa.org/pds/trends.htm (October 2013).
15. Haub, Carl. "Fact Sheet: World Population Trends 2012." Population Reference Bureau. July 2012. http://www.prb.org/Publications/Datasheets/2012/world-population-data-sheet/fact-sheet-world-population.aspx (October 2013).
16. Wise, Jeff. "About That Overpopulation Problem: Research suggests we may actually face a declining world population in the coming years." *Slate*, January 9, 2013. http://www.slate.com/articles/technology/future_tense/2013/01/world_population_may_actually_start_declining_not_exploding.html (October 2013).
17. Harby, Alexandra. "Without Babies, Can Japan Survive?" *The New York Times*, December 15,

2012. http://www.nytimes.com/2012/12/16/opinion/sunday/without-babies-can-japan-survive.html?_r=1& (October 2013).

18. Harby, Alexandra. "Without Babies, Can Japan Survive?" *The New York Times*, December 15, 2012. http://www.nytimes.com/2012/12/16/opinion/sunday/without-babies-can-japan-survive.html?_r=1& (October 2013).

19. U.S. Census Bureau "IDB Aggregation." http://www.census.gov/ipc/www/idbagg.html (September 2004).

20. World Health Organization "Ageing and Life Course: Care and independence in older age." http://www.who.int/ageing/en/ (October 2013).

21. Administrationg on Aging "Aging Statistics." http://www.aoa.gov/Aging_Statistics/ (October 2013)

22. United Nations Department of Economic and Social Affairs Population Division "World Urbanization Prospects: The 2011 Revision." esa.un.org/unup/pdf/WUP2011_Highlights.pdf (October 2013).

23. United Nations Department of Economic and Social Affairs Population Division "World Urbanization Prospects: The 2011 Revision." esa.un.org/unup/pdf/WUP2011_Highlights.pdf (October 2013).

24. United Nations Department of Economic and Social Affairs Population Division "World Urbanization Prospects: The 2011 Revision." esa.un.org/unup/pdf/WUP2011_Highlights.pdf (October 2013).

25. World Atlas "Largest Cities in the World." http://www.worldatlas.com/citypops.htm#.Uhz2NYWsGkI (October 2013).

26. United Nations Department of Economic and Social Affiars Population Division "World Urbanization Prospects: The 2011 Revision." esa.un.org/unup/pdf/WUP2011_Highlights.pdf (October 2013).

27. Scheineson, Andrew. "China's Internal Migrants." *Council on Foreign Relations*, May 14, 2009. http://www.cfr.org/china/chinas-internal-migrants/p12943 (October 2013).

28. Scheineson, Andrew. "China's Internal Migrants." *Council on Foreign Relations*, May 14, 2009. http://www.cfr.org/china/chinas-internal-migrants/p12943 (October 2013).

29. United Nations Department of Economic and Social Affairs Population Division "World Urbanization Prospects: The 2011 Revision." esa.un.org/unup/pdf/WUP2011_Highlights.pdf (October 2013).

30. United Nations Department of Economic and Social Affairs Population Division "World Urbanization Prospects: The 2011 Revision." esa.un.org/unup/pdf/WUP2011_Highlights.pdf (October 2013).

31. Dash, Dipak Kumar. "Delhi and Mumbai in worlds top four urban sprawls." *The Times of India*, October 25, 2012. http://articles.timesofindia.indiatimes.com/2012-10-25/india/34728854_1_eduardo-lopez-moreno-mega-cities-urban-agglomerations (October 2013).

32. "This is Africa's New Biggest City: Lagos, Nigeria, Population 21 Million." *The Atlantic*, July 10, 2012. http://www.theatlantic.com/international/archive/2012/07/this-is-africas-new-biggest-city-lagos-nigeria-population-21-million/259611/ (October 2013).

33. Patrick, Aaron O., Jason Singer and Steve Stecklow. "Watch on the Thames: Surveillance Cameras Monitor Much of Daily Life in London." *The Wall Street Journal*, July 8, 2005. http://online.wsj.com/news/articles/SB112077340647880052 (November 2013).

34. Lock, Cheryl. "The Future of America: 3 Predictions from an Economic Guru." *Forbes*, August 6, 2013. http://www.forbes.com/sites/learnvest/2013/08/06/the-future-of-america-3-predictions-from-an-economic-guru/3/ (November 2013).

35. Harmon, Katherine. "How Black Death Kept Its Genes But Lost Its Killing Power." *The Huffington Post*, October 12, 2011. http://www.huffingtonpost.com/2011/10/12/dna-black-death-genome_n_1007446.html (November 2013).

36. Benedictow, Ole J. "The Black Death: The Greatest Catastrophe Ever." *HistoryToday*, 2005. http://www.historytoday.com/ole-j-benedictow/black-death-greatest-catastrophe-ever (November 2013).

37. Flu.gov "Pandemic Flu History." http://www.flu.gov/pandemic/history# (November 2013)

38. Flu.gov "Pandemic Flu History." http://www.flu.gov/pandemic/history# (November 2013)

39. Begley, Sharon. "Flu-conomics: The next pandemic could trigger global recession." *Reuters*, January 21, 2013. http://www.reuters.com/article/2013/01/21/us-reutersmagazine-davos-flu-economy-idUSBRE90K0F820130121 (November 2013)

40. Bartelme, Tony. "Foreign Water a Growing Worry." The Post and Courier. Jan 19, 1997. http://archives.charleston.net/fish/fish7.html (September 2004).

41. CDC "CDC Telebriefing Transcript: Monkeypox Investigation." June 7, 2003. http://www.cdc.gov/od/oc/media/transcripts/t030607.htm (September 2004).

42. CSIS "World AIDS Summit Warns of Challenges Ahead." September 2002. http://globalization101.org/news.asp?NEWS_ID=35 (September 2004).

43. AIDS.gov "Global Statistics." http://aids.gov/hiv-aids-basics/hiv-aids-101/global-statistics/index.html (November 2013).

44. AVERT "Africa HIV & AIDS Statistics." http://www.avert.org/africa-hiv-aids-statistics.htm

(November 2013).

45. UNAIDS "UNAIDS World AIDS Day Report 2012." http://www.google.com/url?sa=t&rct=-j&q=&esrc=s&source=web&cd=1&ved=0CC4QFjAA&url=http%3A%2F%2Fwww.unaids.org%2Fen%2Fmedia%2Funaids%2Fcontentassets%2Fdocuments%2Fepidemiology%2F2012%2Fgr2012%2Fjc2434_worldaidsday_results_en.pdf&ei=keNvUtXhGLWq4APJ8oDQBA&usg=AFQjCNH3A4f5PzKnRjmRiW1LUl8jCityNw&sig2=ZKXL_kO1lGuRmr9f-5qYUQ&bvm=bv.55123115,d.dmg (November 2013).

46. AIDS.gov "Global Statistics." http://aids.gov/hiv-aids-basics/hiv-aids-101/global-statistics/index.html (November 2013).

47. UNAIDS "UNAIDS World AIDS Day Report 2012." http://www.google.com/url?sa=t&rct=-j&q=&esrc=s&source=web&cd=2&ved=0CEEQFjAB&url=http%3A%2F%2Fwww.unaids.org%2Fen%2Fmedia%2Funaids%2Fcontentassets%2Fdocuments%2Fepidemiology%2F2012%2Fgr2012%2Fjc2434_worldaidsday_results_en.pdf&ei=8eJvUs_4Aa364AOZ4IGQBQ&usg=AFQjCNH3A4f-5PzKnRjmRiW1LUl8jCityNw&sig2=HMk-29WSn17fYsqeSxaUbQ&bvm=bv.55123115,d.dmg (November 2013).

48. Federal Bureau of Investigation "Weapons of Mass Destruction Frequently Asked Questions." http://www.fbi.gov/about-us/investigate/terrorism/wmd/wmd_faqs (November 2013).

49. Department of Homeland Security "Dark Winter Exercise." June 2001. http://www.homelandsecurity.org/darkwinter/index.cfm (September 2004).

50. Lenntech "Specific questions on water quantities." http://www.lenntech.com/specific-questions-water-quantities.htm (November 2013).

51. Lenntech "Specific questions on water quantities." http://www.lenntech.com/specific-questions-water-quantities.htm (November 2013).

52. Water.org "Billions Daily Affected by Water Crisis." http://water.org/water-crisis/one-billion-affected/ (November 2013).

53. The Water Project "Facts About Water: Statistics on the Water Crisis." http://thewaterproject.org/water_stats.php

54. http://www.unwater.org/statistics_use.html (November 2013).

55. James, Tony. "War on water shortage." *Engineering and Technology Magazine*, February 11, 2013. http://eandt.theiet.org/magazine/2013/02/water-world.cfm (November 2013).

56. Michel, David and Amit Pandya. "Troubled Waters: Climate Change, Hydropolitics, and Transboundary Resources." *STIMSON*, 2009. http://www.stimson.org/images/uploads/research-pdfs/Troubled_Waters-Chapter_5_Patterson.pdfhttp://www.globalpolicy.org/the-dark-side-of-natural-resources-st/water-in-conflict.html (November 2013).

57. Pacific Institute "Water Conflict Chronology Timeline." http://www.worldwater.org/conflict/timeline/ (November 2013).

58. University of Michigan "Water Scarcity: Tomorrow's Problem." http://sitemaker.umich.edu/section9group6/solutions (November 2013).

59. Abutu, Alex. "Nigeria: African Countries Tackle Water Scarcity to Combat Climate Change." *Daily Trust*, March 7, 2013. http://allafrica.com/stories/201303071190.html (November 2013).

60. World Hunger Education Service "2013 World Hunger and Poverty Facts and Statistics." http://www.worldhunger.org/articles/Learn/world%20hunger%20facts%202002.htm (November 2013).

61. World Hunger Education Service "2013 World Hunger and Poverty Facts and Statistics." http://www.worldhunger.org/articles/Learn/world%20hunger%20facts%202002.htm (November 2013).

62. World Food Programme "Hunger Statistics." http://www.wfp.org/hunger/stats (November 2013).

63. Institute of Development Studies "Poorest countries lead the fight against hunger and undernutrition." April 11, 2013. http://www.ids.ac.uk/news/poorest-countries-lead-the-fight-against-hunger-and-undernutrition (November 2013).

64. Asia-Pacific Center for Security Studies "Food Security and Political Stability in the Asia-Pacific Region." September 11, 1998. http://www.apcss.org/Publications/Report_Food_Security_98.html (November 2013).

65. Bar-Yam, Y., Bertrand, K.Z. and Lagi, M. "The Food Crises and Political Instability in North Africa and the Middle East." *New England Complex Systems Institute*, August 10, 2011. http://necsi.edu/research/social/foodcrises.html (November 2013).

66. The Organic and Non-GMO Report "Global agriculture report says GM crops not a solution." http://www.non-gmoreport.com/articles/may08/global_agriculture_gm_crops.php (November 2013).

67. World Trade Organization "Doha Development Agenda: Negotiations, implementation and development." http://www.wto.org/english/tratop_e/dda_e/negotiations_summary_e.htm (November 2013).

68. U.S. Energy Information Administration "International Energy Outlook 2013." http://www.eia.

69. Peixe, Joao. "European Parliament Prepares to Discusss Future of Biofuels in the EU." *OilPrice.com*, September 12, 2013. oilprice.com/Latest-Energy-News/World-News/European-Parliament-Prepares-to-Discuss-Future-of-Biofuels-in-the-EU.html (November 2013).

70. Dispatch, Tom. "When will the Clean Energy Future we Dream of Actually Arrive?" *OilPrice.com*, September 10, 2013. http://oilprice.com/Energy/Energy-General/When-will-the-Clean-Energy-Future-we-Dream-of-Actually-Arrive.html (November 2013).

71. Thompson, Loren. "What Happens When America No Longer Needs Middle East Oil?" *Forbes*, December 3, 2012. http://www.forbes.com/sites/lorenthompson/2012/12/03/what-happens-when-america-no-longer-needs-middle-east-oil/ (November 2013).

72. Thompson, Loren. "What Happens When America No Longer Needs Middle East Oil?" *Forbes*, December 3, 2012. ttp://www.forbes.com/sites/lorenthompson/2012/12/03/what-happens-when-america-no-longer-needs-middle-east-oil/ (November 2013).

73. Dispatch, Tom. "When will the Clean Energy Future we Dream of Actually Arrive?" *OilPrice.com*, September 10, 2013. http://oilprice.com/Energy/Energy-General/When-will-the-Clean-Energy-Future-we-Dream-of-Actually-Arrive.html (November 2013).

74. Dispatch, Tom. "When will the Clean Energy Future we Dream of Actually Arrive?" *OilPrice.com*, September 10, 2013. http://oilprice.com/Energy/Energy-General/When-will-the-Clean-Energy-Future-we-Dream-of-Actually-Arrive.html (November 2013).

75. The World Bank "World Development Report 2003: Sustainable Development in a Dynamic World." http://web.worldbank.org/WBSITE/EXTERNAL/EXTDEC/EXTRESEARCH/EXTWDRS/0,,contentMDK:23062331~pagePK:478093~piPK:477627~theSitePK:477624,00.html (November 2013).

76. Bowman, Kerry; Dan Brown; Flavio Comin; Peter Kouwenhover; Ton Manders; Diego Martino; Patrick Milimo; Jennifer Mohamed-Katerere; Thierry De Oliveira; and Zinta Zommers. "Environment for Development." *Section A: Overview.* http://www.unep.org/geo/geo4/report/01_Environment_for_Development.pdf (November 2013).

77. Bowman, Kerry; Dan Brown; Flavio Comin; Peter Kouwenhover; Ton Manders; Diego Martino; Patrick Milimo; Jennifer Mohamed-Katerere; Thierry De Oliveira; and Zinta Zommers. "Environment for Development." *Section A: Overview.* http://www.unep.org/geo/geo4/report/01_Environment_for_Development.pdf (November 2013).

78. The World Bank " 'Climate Smart' World Within Reach, says World Bank." December 2010. http://web.worldbank.org/WBSITE/EXTERNAL/NEWS/0,,contentMDK:22312494~pagePK:64257043~piPK:437376~theSitePK:4607,00.html (November 2013).

79. Harvey, Fiona. "Lord Stern: developing countries must maker deeper emissions cuts." *The Guardian*, December 3, 2012. http://www.theguardian.com/environment/2012/dec/04/lord-stern-developing-countries-deeper-emissions-cuts (November 2013).

80. "China to Start Monitoring Pollution Effects in Worst Hit Cities." Bloomberg News, October 29, 2013. http://www.bloomberg.com/news/2013-10-28/china-to-start-monitoring-pollution-effects-in-worst-hit-cities.html (November 2013).

81. Bowman, Kerry; Dan Brown; Flavio Comin; Peter Kouwenhover; Ton Manders; Diego Martino; Patrick Milimo; Jennifer Mohamed-Katerere; Thierry De Oliveira; and Zinta Zommers. "Environment for Development." *Section A: Overview.* http://www.unep.org/geo/geo4/report/01_Environment_for_Development.pdf (November 2013).

82. The United Nations Framework Convention on Climate Change. http://unfccc.int/text/resource (September 2004).

83. The United Nations Framework Convention on Climate Change. "Kyoto Protocol." http://unfccc.int/kyoto_protocol/items/2830.php (November 2013).

84. U.S. Energy Information Administration "International Energy Statistics." http://www.eia.gov/cfapps/ipdbproject/IEDIndex3.cfm?tid=90&pid=44&aid=8 (November 2013).

85. The World Bank " 'Climate Smart' World Within Reach, says World Bank." December 2010. "http://web.worldbank.org/WBSITE/EXTERNAL/NEWS/0,,contentMDK:22312494~pagePK:64257043~piPK:437376~theSitePK:4607,00.html (November 2013).

86. The Environmental Protection Agency "Clear Skies Plan." http://www.epa.gov/clearskies/ (September 2004).

87. "What is the carbon tax?" *A Daily Wire.* http://www.carbontax.net.au/category/what-is-the-carbon-tax/ (November 2013).

88. "What is the carbon tax?" *A Daily Wire.* http://www.carbontax.net.au/category/what-is-the-carbon-tax/ (November 2013)

89. The Environmental Protection Agency "Clear Skies Plan." http://www.epa.gov/clearskies/ (September 2004).

90. The White House "President Obama's Plan to Fight Climate Change." June 25, 2013. http://www.whitehouse.gov/share/climate-action-plan (November 2013).
91. The White House "President Obama's Plan to Fight Climate Change." June 25 2013. http://www.whitehouse.gov/share/climate-action-plan (November 2013).
92. The White House "President Obama's Plan to Fight Climate Change." June 25, 2013. http://www.whitehouse.gov/share/climate-action-plan (November 2013).
93. The White House "President Obama's Plan to Fight Climate Change." June 25, 2013. http://www.whitehouse.gov/share/climate-action-plan (November 2013).
94. The United Nations Education, Scientific and Cultural Organization "Water Cooperation: Facts and figures." http://www.unwater.org/water-cooperation-2013/water-cooperation/facts-and-figures/en/ (November 2013).
95. The United Nations Education, Scientific and Cutural Organization "The World Water Assessment Program." http://www.unesco.org/water/wwap/facts_figures/index.shtml (September 2004).
96. The United Nations Education, Scientific and Cultural Organization "The World Water Assessment Program." http://www.unesco.org/water/wwap/facts_figures/index.shtml (September 2004).
97. U.S. Environmental Protection Agency "Pollution Prevention (P2)." http://www.epa.gov/p2/pubs/laws.htm (November 2013).
98. Ball, Jeffrey. "Honda, Toyota Plan to Release Fuel-Cell Test Vehicles in the U.S." The Wall Street Journal. Dec. 3, 2002. Pg. D.3
99. Food and Agriculture Organization of the United Nations "Deforestation and net forest area change." http://www.fao.org/forestry/30515/en/ (November 2013).
100. Food and Agriculture Organization of the United Nations "Deforestation and net forest area change." http://www.fao.org/forestry/30515/en/ (November 2013).
101. Daniels, Amy E., Kenneth Bagstad, Valerie Esposito, Azur Moulaert, Carlos Manuel Rodriguez. "Understanding the impacts of Costa Rica's PES: Are we asking the right questions?" *Ecological Economics*, June 3, 2010. www.uvm.edu/giee/pubpdfs/Daniels_2010_Ecological_Economics.pdf (November 2013).
102. Moskvitch, Katia. "Biomining: How microbes help to mine copper." *BBC News*, March 20, 2012. http://www.bbc.co.uk/news/technology-17406375 (November 2013).
103. World Economic Forum "What If the World's Soil Runs Out?" *TIME*, December 14, 2012. http://world.time.com/2012/12/14/what-if-the-worlds-soil-runs-out/ (November 2013).
104. World Economic Forum "What If the World's Soil Runs Out?" *TIME*, December 14, 2012. http://world.time.com/2012/12/14/what-if-the-worlds-soil-runs-out/ (November 2013).
105. World Economic Forum "What If the World's Soil Runs Out?" *TIME*, December 14, 2012. http://world.time.com/2012/12/14/what-if-the-worlds-soil-runs-out/ (November 2013).
106. World Information Transfer "Desertification: Its Effects on People and Land." *World Ecology Report: Critical Issues in Health and Environment*, Spring 2009, Vol. XXI, No. 1. http://worldinfo.org/wp-content/uploads/library/wer/english/2009_Spring_Vol_XXI_no_1.pdf (November 2013).
107. Watts, Jonathan. "China makes gain in battle against disertification but has long fight ahead." *The Guardian*, January 4, 2011. http://www.theguardian.com/world/2011/jan/04/china-desertification (November 2013).
108. United Nations Convention to Combat Desertification. http://www.unccd.int/main.php (September 2004)
109. World Information Transfer "Desertification: Its Effects on People and Land." *World Ecology Report: Critical Issues in Health and Environment*, Spring 2009, Vol. XXI, No. 1. http://worldinfo.org/wp-content/uploads/library/wer/english/2009_Spring_Vol_XXI_no_1.pdf (November 2013).
110. Smith, Tierney. "How Korean organisations combat desertification in Inner Mongolia." *Responding to Climate Change*, April 30, 2012. http://www.rtcc.org/2012/04/26/how-korean-organisations-are-combating-desertification-in-mongolia/ (November 2013).
111. Central Intelligence Agency "The World Factbook." https://www.cia.gov/library/publications/the-world-factbook/geos/xx.html (December 2013).
112. Ghadar, Fariborz. "Economic Intergration: Tech-Enabled Synthesis." *Industrial Management*. http://www.ghadar.com/secondarypages/research/articles/Economic%20Integration-%20Tech-Enabled%20Synthesis.pdf (November 2013).
113. The World Bank "China Overview." http://www.worldbank.org/en/country/china/overview (December 2013)
114. United Nations Conference on Trade and Development "Foreign Direct Investment." http://unctad.org/en/Pages/DIAE/Foreign-Direct-Investment-%28FDI%29.aspx (December 2013)
115. Zhan, James. "Latest Developments in FDI Trends and Policies." *Investment, Enterprise and Development Commission (5th session)*, April 29, 2013. http://unctad.org/Sections/dite_dir/docs/diae_stat_2013-04-29_d2_en.pdf (December 2013).

116. George, Katy; James Manyika and Louis Rassey. "Get Ready for the New Era of Global Manufacturing." *Harvard Business Review Blog Network*, January 13, 2013. http://blogs.hbr.org/2013/01/get-ready-for-the-new-era-of-g/ (December 2013).

117. Ikenson, Daniel. "Made on Earth: How Global Economic Integration Renders Trade Policy Obsolete." *Center for Trade Policy Studies*, December 2, 2009.http://www.cato.org/sites/cato.org/files/pubs/pdf/tpa-042.pdf (December 2013).

118. Boeing "Flying into the Future." http://www.newairplane.com/787/ (December 2013).

119. Kadlec, Dan. "Birth Rate Plumets During Recession." *TIME*, December 4, 2012. http://business.time.com/2012/12/04/birth-rate-plunges-during-recession/ (December 2013).

120. "Jagdish Bhagwati Testimony: Subcommittee on Domestic and International Monetary Policy, Trade and Technology." April 1, 2003. http://financialservices.house.gov/media/pdf/040103jb.pdf (September 2004).

121. King, Neil and Scott Miller. "Trade Talks Fail Amid Big Divide Over Farm Issues; Developing Countries Object to U.S., EU Goals; Cotton as a Rallying Cry." *The Wall Street Journal*. (Eastern edition). Sept. 15, 2003. pg. A1.

122. Dearaujo, Ernani. "Chaotic Congo." *Harvard International Review*. Cambridge, Fall 2011. Vol. 23, Iss. 3, pg. 10.

123. Organisation for Economic Co-Operation and Development Paris 1996 "The Knowledge-Based Economy." http://www.google.com/url?sa=t&rct=j&q=&esrc=s&source=web&cd=5&ved=0CFgQ-FjAE&url=http%3A%2F%2Fwww.oecd.org%2Fdataoecd%2F51%2F8%2F1913021.pdf&ei=BrRxUuezLsL-C4APTrIDoBg&usg=AFQjCNGYDTzONvf7cgvAWMpShRiI3_6sdA&sig2=quHvmedn0WRJIvMaGMqv-vw&bvm=bv.55819444,d.dmg (December 2013).

124. Whipps, Heather. "How Gunpowder Changed the World." *LiveScience*, April 6, 2008. http://www.livescience.com/7476-gunpowder-changed-world.html (December 2013).

125. The Emmy Foundation Archive of American Television "A Brief History of Television." http://www.emmytvlegends.org/resources/tv-history (December 2013).

126. *The Rise and Fall of the K-Drama Empire*. http://withs2.com/wp-content/uploads/2011/01/The-Rise-and-Fall-of-the-K-Drama-Empire-Chapter-2-Mad-Men.pdf (December 2013).

127. "Radio and Television." *History*. http://www.history.com/topics/radio-and-television (December 2013).

128. The Emmy Foundation Archive of American Television "A Brief History of Television." http://www.emmytvlegends.org/resources/tv-history (December 2013).

129. Etherington, Darrell. "Apple's iPhone 5s and iPhone 5c Sell 9M Units Over Opening Weekend, Topping 5M for iPhone 5 Last Year." *TechCrunch*, September 23, 2013. http://techcrunch.com/2013/09/23/apples-iphone-5s-and-iphone-5c-sell-9m-units-over-opening-weekend-topping-5m-for-iphone-5-last-year/ (December 2013).

130. DeGusta, Michael. "Are Smart Phones Spreading Faster than Any Technology in Human History?" *MIT Technology Review*, May 9, 2012. http://www.technologyreview.com/news/427787/are-smart-phones-spreading-faster-than-any-technology-in-human-history/page/2/ (December 2013).

131. Seven Sisters Sheep Centre "The Hisotry of British Wool." http://www.sheepcentre.co.uk/wool.htm (December 2013).

132. Gillard, Derek. *Education in England: a brief history* (2011). http://www.educationengland.org.uk/history/chapter02.html (December 2013).

133. Naughton, Keith. "Outsourcing: Silicon Valley East." *Newsweek*, March 6, 2006. http://www.cs.rice.edu/~vardi/newsweek.html (December 2013).

134. Ghadar, Fariborz. "Knowledge Dissemination: Economic Development Solution." *Industrial Management*. http://www.ghadar.com/secondarypages/research/articles/Knowledge%20Dissemination%20-%20Economic%20Development%20Solution.pdf (November 2013).

135. Friedman, Thomas. "The Truth about the Flat World, Part One." *Think Tank with Ben Wattenberg*, June 23, 2005. http://www.pbs.org/thinktank/transcript1189.html (December 2013).

136. Ghadar, Fariborz. "Knowledge Dissemination: Economic Development Solution." *Industrial Management*. http://www.ghadar.com/secondarypages/research/articles/Knowledge%20Dissemination%20-%20Economic%20Development%20Solution.pdf (November 2013).

137. Ghadar, Fariborz. "Knowledge Dissemination: Economic Development Solution." *Industrial Management*. http://www.ghadar.com/secondarypages/research/articles/Knowledge%20Dissemination%20-%20Economic%20Development%20Solution.pdf (November 2013).

138. Ghadar, Fariborz. "Knowledge Dissemination: Economic Development Solution. *Industrial Management*. http://www.ghadar.com/secondarypages/research/articles/Knowledge%20Dissemination%20-%20Economic%20Development%20Solution.pdf (November 2013).

139. Campbell, Joel R. "Becoming a Techno-Industrial Power: Chinese Science and Technology

140. Policy." *Brookings*, April 29 2013. http://www.brookings.edu/research/papers/2013/04/29-science-technology-policy-china-campbell (December 2013).

140. Ghadar, Fariborz. "Knowledge Dissemination: Economic Development Solution." *Industrial Management*. http://www.ghadar.com/secondarypages/research/articles/Knowledge%20Dissemination%20-%20Economic%20Development%20Solution.pdf (November 2013).

141. "China shows determination to increase education fund." *People's Daily Online*, March 8, 2013. http://english.peopledaily.com.cn/90778/8159639.html (December 2013).

142. Ghadar, Fariborz. "Knowledge Dissemination: Economic Development Solution." *Industrail Management*. http://www.ghadar.com/secondarypages/research/articles/Knowledge%20Dissemination%20-%20Economic%20Development%20Solution.pdf (November 2013).

143. RAND Corporation "Linking Funding and Quality to Improve Higher Education in India." http://www.rand.org/pubs/research_briefs/RB9720/index1.html (December 2013).

144. RAND Corporation "Linking Funding and Quality to Improve Higher Education in India." http://www.rand.org/pubs/research_briefs/RB9720/index1.html (December 2013).

145. Agarwal, Pawan and Philip G. Altback. "Scoring higher on education." *The Hindu*, February 12, 2013. http://www.thehindu.com/opinion/op-ed/scoring-higher-on-education/article4404687.ece (December 2013).

146. Karnik, Kiran. "Indian IT industry revenues set to cross $100 billion." *The Economic Times*, March 7, 2012. http://articles.economictimes.indiatimes.com/2012-03-07/news/31132044_1_private-sector-higher-education-sector-new-technologies (December 2013).

147. India Brand Equity Foundation "IT & ITeS Industry in India." December 2013. http://www.ibef.org/industry/information-technology-india.aspx (December 2013).

148. Ghadar, Fariborz. "Knowledge Dissemination: Economic Development Solution." *Industrial Management*. http://www.ghadar.com/secondarypages/research/articles/Knowledge%20Dissemination%20-%20Economic%20Development%20Solution.pdf (November 2013).

149. Ghadar, Fariborz. "Knowledge Dissemination: Economic Development Solution." *Industrial Management*. http://www.ghadar.com/secondarypages/research/articles/Knowledge%20Dissemination%20-%20Economic%20Development%20Solution.pdf (November 2013).

150. Ghadar, Fariborz. "Knoweledge Dissemination: Economic Development Solution." *Industrial Management*. http://www.ghadar.com/secondarypages/research/articles/Knowledge%20Dissemination%20-%20Economic%20Development%20Solution.pdf (November 2013).

151. Organisation for Economic Co-Operation and Development Paris 1996 "The Knowledge-Based Economy." http://www.google.com/url?sa=t&rct=j&q=&esrc=s&source=web&cd=5&ved=0CFgQ-FjAE&url=http%3A%2F%2Fwww.oecd.org%2Fdataoecd%2F51%2F8%2F1913021.pdf&ei=BrRxUuezLsL-C4APTrIDoBg&usg=AFQjCNGYDTzONvf7cgvAWMpShRiI3_6sdA&sig2=quHvmedn0WRJIvMaGMqv-vw&bvm=bv.55819444,d.dmg (December 2013).

152. Greenberg, Samuel. "The Future of IT." *CIO Insight*, January 23, 2012. http://www.cioinsight.com/it-management/innovation/the-future-of-it (December 2013).

153. Internet World Stats "Internet Users in the World Distribution by World Regions - 2012 Q2." http://www.internetworldstats.com/stats.htm (December 2013).

154. Greenberg, Samuel. "The Future of IT." *CIO Insight*, January 23, 2013. http://www.cioinsight.com/it-management/innovation/the-future-of-it#sthash.kD8V7BfL.dpuf (December 2013).

155. Greenberg, Samuel. "The Future of IT." *CIO Insight*, January 23, 2013. http://www.cioinsight.com/it-management/innovation/the-future-of-it#sthash.kD8V7BfL.dpuf (December 2013).

156. Healey, James R. and Kelsey Mays. "Which cars park themselves best? Challenge results." *USA Today*, December 6, 2012. http://www.usatoday.com/story/money/cars/2012/12/06/self-parking-cars-challenge/1743199/ (December 2013).

157. Irwin, Neil. "These 12 technologies will drive our economic future." *The Washington Post*, May 24, 2013. http://www.washingtonpost.com/blogs/wonkblog/wp/2013/05/24/these-12-technologies-will-drive-our-economic-future/ (December 2013).

158. Greenberg, Samuel. "The Future of IT." *CIO Insight*, January 23, 2013. http://www.cioinsight.com/it-management/innovation/the-future-of-it-3/#sthash.1qEb3VWV.dpuf (December 2013).

159. World Economic Forum "Global Information Technology Report 2013." http://www.weforum.org/reports/global-information-technology-report-2013#egovernment (December 2013)

160. World Economic Forum "Global Information Technology Report 2013." http://www.weforum.org/reports/global-information-technology-report-2013#egovernment (December 2013).

161. World Economic Forum "Global Information Technology Report 2013." http://www.weforum.org/reports/global-information-technology-report-2013#egovernment (December 2013).

162. The Center for Future Studies "Science and Technology Overview." 1999. htttp://www.future-studies.co.uk/predictions/099.pdf (September 2004).

163. World Economic Forum. "Global Information Technology Report 2013." http://www.weforum.org/reports/global-information-technology-report-2013#egovernment (December 2013).
164. Friedrich, Otto. "The Robot Revolution." *Time*, Dec. 8, 1980.
165. National Aeronautics and Space Administration NASA Science "Missions - Mars Exploration Rover - Opportunity - NASA Science." Apr. 30, 2013. http://science.nasa.gov/missions/mars-rovers/ (February 2014).
166. Worstall, Tim. "Phew, The Robots Are Only Going To Take 45 Percent Of All The Jobs." *Forbes*, Sept. 18, 2013. http://www.forbes.com/sites/timworstall/2013/09/18/phew-the-robots-are-only-going-to-take-45-percent-of-all-the-jobs/ (January 2014).
167. Larson, Christina. "China Expected to Be the Top Market for Industrial Robots by 2016." Bloomberg.com. Nov. 15, 2013. http://www.businessweek.com/articles/2013-11-15/china-expected-to-be-top-market-for-industrial-robots-by-2016 (January 2014).
168. Larson, Christina. "China Expected to Be the Top Market for Industrial Robots by 2016." Bloomberg.com. Nov. 15, 2013. http://www.businessweek.com/articles/2013-11-15/china-expected-to-be-top-market-for-industrial-robots-by-2016 (January 2014).
169. Larson, Christina. "China Expected to Be the Top Market for Industrial Robots by 2016." Bloomberg.com. Nov. 15, 2013. http://www.businessweek.com/articles/2013-11-15/china-expected-to-be-top-market-for-industrial-robots-by-2016 (January 2014).
170. Aquino, Judith. "Nine Jobs That Humans May Lose to Robots." Msnbc.com. http://www.nbcnews.com/id/42183592/ns/business-careers/t/nine-jobs-humans-may-lose-robots/#.UuU1y7Qo7IU (January 2014).
171. Lanfranco, Anthony, BAS, Andres Castellanos, MD, Jaydev Desai, PhD, and William Meyers, MD. "Robotic Surgery." National Center for Biotechnology Information. US National Library of Medicine, Jan. 2004. http://www.ncbi.nlm.nih.gov/pmc/articles/PMC1356187/ (January 2014).
172. UCLA David Geffen School of Medicine. "Future of Surgery." http://casit.ucla.edu/body.cfm?id=6 (January 2014).
173. McCabe, Liam, Keith Barry, and Tyler W. Lynch. "A Thinking Refrigerator? Smart Kitchens Are Coming." *USA Today*, Apr. 8, 2013. http://www.usatoday.com/story/money/business/2013/04/08/high-tech-home-improvement-kitchens/2043807/ (January 2014).
174. McCabe, Liam, Keith Barry, and Tyler W. Lynch. "A Thinking Refrigerator? Smart Kitchens Are Coming." *USA Today*, Apr. 8, 2013. <http://www.usatoday.com/story/money/business/2013/04/08/high-tech-home-improvement-kitchens/2043807/ (January 2014).
175. Markoff, John. "Google Cars Drive Themselves, in Traffic." *The New York Times*, Oct. 9, 2009.
176. Kelly, Heather. "Driverless Car Tech Gets Serious at CES." *CNN*, Jan. 9, 2014.
177. Kelly, Heather. "Driverless Car Tech Gets Serious at CES." *CNN*, Jan. 9, 2014.
178. Worstall, Tim. "Don't Tell The Teamsters: But Driverless Trucks Are Already Here." *Forbes Magazine*, Nov. 26, 2012. http://www.forbes.com/sites/timworstall/2012/11/26/dont-tell-the-teamsters-but-driverless-trucks-are-already-here/ (February 2014).
179. Geron, Tomio. "Uber Confirms $258 Million From Google Ventures, TPG, Looks To On-Demand Future." *Forbes Magazine*, Aug. 23, 2013. http://www.forbes.com/sites/tomiogeron/2013/08/23/uber-confirms-258-million-from-google-ventures-tpg-looks-to-on-demand-future/ (February 2014).
180. Uber "Uber." https://www.uber.com/ (February 2014).
181. Markoff, John. "Google Adds to Its Managerie of Robots." *New York Times*, Dec. 14, 2013. http://www.nytimes.com/2013/12/14/technology/google-adds-to-its-menagerie-of-robots.html (February 2014).
182. Barr, Alistair. "Amazon Testing Delivery by Drone, CEO Bezos Says." *USA Today*, Dec. 2, 2013.
183. Barr, Alistair. "Amazon Testing Delivery by Drone, CEO Bezos Says." *USA Today*, Dec. 2, 2013.
184. Uber "Uber." https://www.uber.com/ (February 2014).
185. "This Is Your Ground Pilot Speaking." *The Economist*, Nov., 24 2012.
186. "This Is Your Ground Pilot Speaking." *The Economist*, Nov., 24 2012.
187. "This Is Your Ground Pilot Speaking." *The Economist*, Nov., 24 2012.
188. Dobbs, Taylor. "Farms of the Future Will Run on Robots and Drones." *PBS*, Jan. 9, 2013. http://www.pbs.org/wgbh/nova/next/tech/farming-with-robotics-automation-and-sensors/ (February 2014).
189. Geron, Tomio. "Uber Confirms $258 Million From Google Ventures, TPG, Looks To On-Demand Future." *Forbes Magazine*, Aug. 23, 2013. http://www.forbes.com/sites/tomiogeron/2013/08/23/uber-confirms-258-million-from-google-ventures-tpg-looks-to-on-demand-future/ (February 2014).
190. "U.S. Army General Says Robots Could Replace One-fourth of Combat Soldiers by 2030." *CBSNews*. CBS Interactive, Jan. 23 2014. http://www.cbsnews.com/news/robotic-soldiers-by-2030-us-army-general-says-robots-may-replace-combat-soldiers/ (February 2014).
191. "U.S. Army General Says Robots Could Replace One-fourth of Combat Soldiers by 2030." *CBSNews*. CBS Interactive, Jan. 23 2014. http://www.cbsnews.com/news/robotic-soldiers-by-2030-us-ar-

my-general-says-robots-may-replace-combat-soldiers/ (February 2014).

192. "U.S. Army General Says Robots Could Replace One-fourth of Combat Soldiers by 2030." *CBSNews*. CBS Interactive, Jan. 23 2014. http://www.cbsnews.com/news/robotic-soldiers-by-2030-us-army-general-says-robots-may-replace-combat-soldiers/ (February 2014).

193. Sifferlin, Alexandra. "FDA approves first bionic eye." *CNN Health*, February 19, 2013. http://www.cnn.com/2013/02/19/health/fda-bionic-eye (September 2013).

194. Armstrong, Doree and Michelle Ma. "Researcher controls colleague's motions in 1st human brain-to-brain interface." University of Washington, April 27, 2013. http://www.washington.edu/news/2013/08/27/researcher-controls-colleagues-motions-in-1st-human-brain-to-brain-interface/ (September 2013).

195. Oregon Health & Science University "OHSU AIDS vaccine candidate appears to completely clear virus from body." September 11, 2013. http://www.ohsu.edu/xd/about/news_events/news/2013/09-11-ohsu-vaccine-candidate-a.cfm%20?utm_campaign=240_CloserToACure_1.jpg&utm_source=homebanner&WT.ac=240_CloserToACure_1.jpg&WT.ac=240_CloserToACure_1 (September 2013).

196. Plunkett Research, Ltd. "The State of the Biotechnology Industry Today." http://www.plunkettresearch.com/biotech-drugs-genetics-market-research/industry-and-business-data (September 2013).

197. *Scientific American World View A Global Biotechnology Perspective*. http://www.saworldview.com//wv/assets/SAWorldView2013_Final.pdf (September 2013).

198. Herper, Matthew. "The Best- and Worst-Performing Biotech Stocks July 26 to August 2." *Forbes*, August 4, 2013. http://www.forbes.com/sites/matthewherper/2013/08/04/the-best-and-worst-performing-biotech-stocks-july-26-to-august-2/ (September 2013).

199. Plunkett Research, Ltd. "The State of the Biotechnology Industry Today. http://www.plunkettresearch.com/biotech-drugs-genetics-market-research/industry-and-business-data (September 2013).

200. EuropaBio *Healthcare Manifesto 2011-2012*. http://www.europabio.org/sites/default/files/position/europabio_healthcare_manifesto_2011-2012.pdf (September 2013).

201. Loftus, Peter and Jonathan R. Rockoff. "Pfizer Pushes on New Biotech Drugs." *The Wall Street Journal*, April 28, 2010. http://online.wsj.com/article/SB10001424052748704464704575208580328253618.html (September 2013).

202. International Service for the Acquisition of Agri-Biotech "Top Ten Facts about Biotech/GM Crops in 2012: A new overview of biotech crops in 2012." https://www.isaaa.org/resources/publications/briefs/44/toptenfacts/default.asp (September 2013).

203. Dunmore, Charles. "Monsanto to grow European seed business after GMO pullout." *Reuters*, July 18, 2013. http://www.reuters.com/article/2013/07/18/monsanto-europe-idUSL6N0FO3TB20130718 (September 2013).

204. International Service for the Acquisition of Agri-Biotech "Top Ten Facts about Biotech/GM Crops in 2012: A new overview of biotech crops in 2012." https://www.isaaa.org/resources/publications/briefs/44/toptenfacts/default.asp (September 2013).

205. International Service for the Acquisition of Agri-Biotech "Top Ten Facts about Biotech/GM Crops in 2012: A new overview of biotech crops in 2012." https://www.isaaa.org/resources/publications/briefs/44/toptenfacts/default.asp (September 2013).

206. International Service for the Acquisition of Agri-Biotech "Top Ten Facts about Biotech/GM Crops in 2012: A new overview of biotech crops in 2012." http://www.isaaa.org/resources/publications/pocketk/16/ (September 2013).

207. Weise, Elizabeth. "Genetically engineered foods Q & A." *USA Today*, October 28, 2012. http://www.usatoday.com/story/news/nation/2012/10/28/gmo-questions/1658225/ (September 2013).

208. MNN HOLDINGS, LLC. "Mad science." Mother Nature Network. http://www.mnn.com/greentech/research-innovations/photos/12-bizarre-examples-of-genetic-engineering/mad-science# (January 2014).

209. Ghadar, Fariborz and Heather Spindler. "The Growth of Biotechnology." *Industrial Management*. March/April 2005.

210. "DuPont to Acquire Danisco for $6.3 Billion." DuPont. http://investors.dupont.com/phoenix.zhtml?c=73320&p=irol-newsArticle&id=1514276 (January 2014).

211. Synthetic Genomics, Inc.. "Alliance between Synthetic Genomics Inc and ExxonMobil Research and Engineering Company." Synthetic Genomics. http://www.syntheticgenomics.com/images/AlgalBiofuelsFactSheet.pdf (January 2014).

212. Science X network. "To clean up the mine, let Ascomycete fungus reproduce." Phys.org. http://phys.org/news/2012-07-ascomycete-fungus.html (January 2014).

213. United Nations. "Population Ageing: A Celebration and a Challenge." United Nations Population Fund. http://www.unfpa.org/pds/ageing.html (January 2014).

214. PMGroup Worldwide Ltd. "Interview: Stephan Tanda, EuropaBio." PMLive. http://www.pmlive.

com/pharma_thought_leadership/interview_stephan_tanda,_europabio_390623 (January 2014).

215. EBD GmbH. "China's rapid growth nourishes biotech environment." partneringNEWS. http://ebdgroup.com/partneringnews/2013/05/china%E2%80%99s-rapid-growth-nourishes-biotech-environment/ (January 2014).

216. "Children Creating Real Objects With Their Mind." Indiegogo. http://www.indiegogo.com/projects/children-creating-real-objects-with-their-mind (January 2014).

217. IBT Media Inc. "3D Printing Powered Only By Thoughts On Scientific Horizon, Still Can't Compete With 'Three Million Dollar Magnet' Of MRI." Medical Daily. http://www.medicaldaily.com/3d-printing-powered-only-thoughts-scientific-horizon-still-cant-compete-three-million-dollar-magnet (January 2014).

218. Handwerk, Brian. "Five Incredible — And Real — Mind Control Applications." *National Geographic*. Aug. 29, 2013. http://news.nationalgeographic.com/news/2013/08/130829-mind-brain-control-robot-brainwave-eeg-3d-printing-music/ (January 2014).

219. "Cyborg Parts ." MIT Technology Review. http://www.technologyreview.com/demo/517991/cyborg-parts (January 2014).

220. United Nations "World Economic and Social Survey 201." http://www.un.org/en/development/desa/policy/wess/wess_current/2011wess.pdf (January 2014)

221. Harmon, Amy . "Golden Rice: Lifesaver?." The New York Times. http://www.nytimes.com/2013/08/25/sunday-review/golden-rice-lifesaver.html?pagewanted=all&_r=2& (January 2014).

222. American Chemical Society. "Toward A Banana-based Vaccine For Hepatitis B." ScienceDaily. www.sciencedaily.com/releases/2007/04/070430224426.htm (January 2014).

223. London South East. "AquaBounty Technologies Net Loss Narrows, Expects US Approval For Fast-Growing Salmon." Alliance News. http://www.lse.co.uk/AllNews.asp?code=9jxwqj3k&headline=AquaBounty_Technologies_Net_Loss_Narrows_Expects_US_Approval_For_FastGrowing_Salmon (January 2014).

224. Crain Communications Ltd . "Industrial biotech market to grow 20% a year." Plastics and Rubber Weekly. http://www.prw.com/subscriber/headlines2.html?cat=1&id=3505 (January 2014).

225. Ghadar, Fariborz, John Sviokla, and Dietrich A Stephan. "Why Life Science Needs Its Own Silicon Valley - Harvard Business Review." Harvard Business Review Magazine, Case Studies, Articles, Books, Pamphlets - Harvard Business Review. Accessed July 9, 2013. http://hbr.org/2012/07/why-life-science-needs-its-own-silicon-valley/ar/1.

226. Ghadar, Fariborz, John Sviokla, and Dietrich A Stephan. "Why Life Science Needs Its Own Silicon Valley - Harvard Business Review." Harvard Business Review Magazine, Case Studies, Articles, Books, Pamphlets - Harvard Business Review. Accessed July 9, 2013. http://hbr.org/2012/07/why-life-science-needs-its-own-silicon-valley/ar/1.

227. Conde Nast Digital. "AI Could Help Predict Which Flu Virus Will Cause the Next Deadly Human Outbreak." Wired.com. http://www.wired.com/wiredscience/2013/09/artificial-intelligence-flu-outbreak/ (January 2014).

228. Singer, Emily. "AI Could Help Predict Which Flu Virus Will Cause the Next Deadly Human Outbreak." Wired. http://www.wired.com/wiredscience/2013/09/artificial-intelligence-flu-outbreak/ (January 2014).

229. Biotechnology Industry Organization . "Five international biotech countries to watch." BIOtechNow. http://www.biotech-now.org/business-and-investments/2011/06/five-international-biotech-countries-to-watch# (January 2014).

230. McBride, Ryan. "Pfizer shares software for biotech drug research with pharma rivals." FierceBiotechIT. http://www.fiercebiotechit.com/story/pfizer-lends-software-biotech-drug-research-pharma-rivals/2013-06-24 (January 2014).

231. Coxworth, Ben. "Researchers grow human brains in a lab." Gizmag. http://www.gizmag.com/lab-grown-mini-brains/28870/ (January 2014).

232. United States National Nanotechnology Initiative. "Size of the Nanoscale." National Nanotechnology Institute. http://www.nano.gov/nanotech-101/what/nano-size (January 2014).

233. Ghadar, Fariborz and Heather Spindler. "Nanotechnogy: Small Revoultion." *Industrial Management*. May/June 2005.

234. Ghadar, Fariborz and Heather Spindler. "Nanotechnogy: Small Revolution." *Industrial Management*. May/June 2005.

235. Harvard Medical School Newsletter *Harvard Health Publications*. Vol. 3, Iss. 9, June 15, 2006 http://harvardhealth.staywell.com/viewNewsletter.aspx?NLID=52&INC=yes (January 2014).

236. Ghadar, Fariborz and Heather Spindler. "Nanotechnogy: Small Revolution." *Industrial Management*. May/June 2005.

237. Jack Uldrich and Deb Newberry, The Next Big Thing Is Really Small: How Nanotechnology Will Change The Future Of Your Business (New York, Random House, Inc., 2003)

238. Hersam, M.C., C.A. Mirkin, and M.C. Roco. "Restrospective and Outlook." Nanotechnology Research Directions for Societal Needs in 2020, Septemner 2010. http://www.wtec.org/nano2/Nanotechnology_Research_Directions_to_2020/.

239. "Nanoscale Science." UNC Charlotte College of Liberal Arts and Sciences. Accessed July 1, 2013. www.google.com/url?sa=t&rct=j&q=&esrc=s&source=web&cd=4&ved=0CEYQFjAD&url=http%3A%2F%2Fnanoscalescience.uncc.edu%2Fdocs%2FNanotech%-2520Decade%2520ChemWorld%2520UK%2520Mar2011%2520%282%29.pdf&ei=7aFCT_3aLIfn0QGxq_yLAg&usg=AFQjCNGlwckjRf4kKkbJhnc61zyNccQ4wg.

240. Georgia Institute of Technology. "Researchers Help Assess Economic Impact of Nanotechnology on Green & Sustainable Growth." Georgia Institute of Technology. http://www.news.gatech.edu/2012/03/27/researchers-help-assess-economic-impact-nanotechnology-green-sustainable-growth (January 2014).

241. "MarketWatch." MarketWatch - Stock Market Quotes, Business News, Financial News. Accessed July 9, 2013. http://www.marketwatch.com/story/global-nanotechnology-industry-output-expected-to-reach-24-trillion-by-2015-2011-11-17.

242. Georgia Institute of Technology. "Researchers Help Assess Economic Impact of Nanotechnology on Green & Sustainable Growth." Georgia Institute of Technology. http://www.news.gatech.edu/2012/03/27/researchers-help-assess-economic-impact-nanotechnology-green-sustainable-growth (January 2014).

243. The Pew Charitable Trusts. "Nanotechnology: Will It Drive a New Innovation Economy for the U.S.? - The Pew Charitable Trusts." The Pew Charitable Trusts. http://www.pewtrusts.org/events_detail.aspx?id=49832 (January 2014).

244. Hadlington, Simon. "Nanotech patent jungle set to become denser in 2013." Royal Society of Chemistry. http://www.rsc.org/chemistryworld/2013/01/nanotechnology-patent-thicket-jungle-graphene-nanotubes (January 2014).

245. Hadlington, Simon. "Nanotech patent jungle set to become denser in 2013." Royal Society of Chemistry. http://www.rsc.org/chemistryworld/2013/01/nanotechnology-patent-thicket-jungle-graphene-nanotubes (January 2014).

246. Dodson, Brian. "Metamaterials breakthrough could lead to the first wide-spectrum optical invisibility cloak ." Gizmag | New and Emerging Technology News. Accessed July 9, 2013. http://www.gizmag.com/metamaterials-wide-spectrum-optical-invisibility-cloak-stanford/27813/.

247. Ghadar, Fariborz and Heather Spindler. "Nanotechnology: Small Revolution." *Industrial Management.* May/June 2005.

248. Anthony, Sebastian. "The first flexible, fiber-optic solar cell that can be woven into clothes | ExtremeTech." Latest Technology News | Tech Blog | ExtremeTech. Accessed July 9, 2013. http://www.extremetech.com/computing/142755-the-first-flexible-fiber-optic-solar-cell-that-can-be-woven-into-clothes.

249. Evan, Donalds. *Values in Medicine: What are We Really Doing to Patients?* Taylor & Francis, Dec. 7 2007.

250. "Nanotechnology - The Future is Coming Sooner Than You Think." Joint Economic Committee Republicans. http://www.bibliotecapleyades.net/ciencia/ciencia_nanotechnology01.htm (January 2014).

251. Ghadar, Fariborz and Heather Spindler. "Nanotechnology: Small Revolution." *Industrial Management.* May/June 2005.

252. World Future Society. "Forecasts From The Futurist magazine." World Future Society. http://www.wfs.org/Forecasts_From_The_Futurist_Magazine (January 2014).

253. 33rd Square. "Future Implications Of Nanotechnology." 33rd Square. http://www.33rdsquare.com/2012/11/future-implications-of-nanotechnology.html (January 2014).

254. "Why Mercury is More Dangerous in Oceans." PRATT SCHOOL OF ENGINEERING CIVIL + ENVIRONMENTAL ENGINEERING. http://www.pratt.duke.edu/sites/pratt.duke.edu/files/CEE-newsletter-2011.pdf (January 2014).

255. Slaughter, Anne-Marie. "Remarks, The Big Picture: Beyond Hot Spots & Crises in Our Interconnected World* ." Penn State Journal of Law & International Affairs 1, no. 2 (2012): 286-302.

256. Hoffman, Frank. "Conflict in the 21st Century: The Rise of Hybrid Wars." Potomac Institute for Policy Studies. http://www.projectwhitehorse.com/pdfs/HybridWar_0108.pdf (January 2014).

257. NCTC. "Terrorist Groups - Hizballah." The National Counterterrorism Center. http://www.nctc.gov/site/groups/hizballah.html (January 2014).

258. Slaughter, Anne-Marie. "Remarks, The Big Picture: Beyond Hot Spots & Crises in Our Interconnected World* ." Penn State Journal of Law & International Affairs 1, no. 2 (2012): 286-302.

259. GlobalSecurity.org. "The World at War." GlobalSecurity. http://www.globalsecurity.org/military/

world/war (January 2014).

260. Hoffman, Frank. "Conflict in the 21st Century: The Rise of Hybrid Wars." Potomac Institute for Policy Studies. http://www.projectwhitehorse.com/pdfs/HybridWar_0108.pdf (January 2014).

261. Ghadar, Fariborz. "Conflict: Its Changing Face." *Industrial Management*. November/December 2006.

262. Polachek, Solomon W., and Daria Sevastianova. "Does Conflict Disrupt Growth? Evidence of the Relationship between Political Instability and National Economic Performance." The Institute for the Study of Labor. http://ftp.iza.org/dp4762.pdf (January 2014).

263. OECD. "Think global, act global: Confronting global factors that influence conflict and fragility." OECD. http://www.oecd.org/dac/incaf/Think_global_act_global_Synthesis_120912_graphics_final.pdf (January 2014).

264. OECD. "Think global, act global: Confronting global factors that influence conflict and fragility." OECD. http://www.oecd.org/dac/incaf/Think_global_act_global_Synthesis_120912_graphics_final.pdf (January 2014).

265. Cooper, Michael , Michael S Schmidt , and Eric Schmitt. "Bombing Suspect Cites Islamic Extremist Beliefs as Motive." The New York Times. Accessed July 24, 2013. http://www.nytimes.com/2013/04/24/us/boston-marathon-bombing-developments.html?pagewanted=all&_r=0.

266. Hoffman, Frank. "Conflict in the 21st Century: The Rise of Hybrid Wars." Potomac Institute for Policy Studies. http://www.projectwhitehorse.com/pdfs/HybridWar_0108.pdf (January 2014).

267. Hayes, Harry. "The Costs of Terrorism." International Review. Jan. 29, 2002. http://www.geocities.com/Paris/Rue/4637/terr25a.html (October 2004).

268. "The Costs of Terrorism." Asia Pacific Economic Cooperation: Submitted by Australia, 2003/SOMI/04. February 2003. http://www.apecsec.org.sg/apec/apec_groups/som_special_task_groups/counter_terrorism.downloadlinks.0007.LinkURL.Download.ver5.1.9 (October 2004).

269. Reuters. "Aramco Says Cyberattack Was Aimed at Production." *The New York Times*. Dec. 9 2012. http://www.nytimes.com/2012/12/10/business/global/saudi-aramco-says-hackers-took-aim-at-its-production.html (December 2013).

270. Smith, Gerry. "Hackers Cost U.S. Economy Up To 500,000 Jobs Each Year, Study Finds." The Huffington Post. http://www.huffingtonpost.com/2013/07/25/hackers-jobs_n_3652893.html (January 2014).

271. U.S. Department of State, United States Embassy, Bogota, Colombia. http://usembassy.state.gov/colombia/wwwsfyi7.shtml (September 2004).

272. Lord Desai, Lord Judd and Sir John Thompson. "Global Governance: Yes, But What, Who and How?" Overseas Development Institute. 1998. http://www.odi.org.uk/speeches/govmt1.html (September 2004).

273. "Corporate Clout 2013: Time for Responsible Capitalism." Global Trends. http://www.global-trends.com/knowledge-center/features/shapers-and-influencers/190-corporate-clout-2013-time-for-responsible-capitalism (January 2014).

274. White, Peter and Beatrijs Buyle. "Corporate Social Opportunity: Sevel Steps to Make Corporate Social Responsibility Work for Your Business." Green Leaf. 2004.

275. Schumpeter. "The Corruption Eruption."The Economist, April 29, 2010. http://www.economist.com/node/16005114 (January 2014).

276. Statista. "Number of NGOs worldwide up to 2010." Statista. http://www.statista.com/statistics/268357/changes-in-the-number-of-ngos-worldwide-since-1948/ (January 2014).

277. "NGO." NGO. http://www.ngo.in/ (January 2014).

278. Leverty , Sally. "NGOs, the UN and APA." American Psychological Association. http://www.apa.org/international/united-nations/publications.aspx (January 2014).

279. Willetts, Peter. "What is a Non-Governmental Organization?." City University London. http://www.staff.city.ac.uk/p.willetts/CS-NTWKS/NGO-ART.HTM (January 2014).

280. Clinton, Hillary. "Internet Rights & Wrongs: Choices and Challenges in a Networked World." Speech, The George Washington University, Feb. 15, 2001.

281. Norton, Quinn. "How Anonymous Picks Targets, Launches Attacks, and Takes Powerful Organizations Down." Wired.com. http://www.wired.com/threatlevel/2012/07/ff_anonymous/ (January 2014).

282. Peters, Jonathan W.. "Op-Ed: WikiLeaks Shows Need for a Legal 'Watchdog Privilege'." Wired.com. http://www.wired.com/threatlevel/2011/05/oped-wikipriviledge/ (January 2014).

Image Sources for Technology Timelines:

Information Technology:
http://www.computermuseum.li/Testpage/IBM-360-1964.htm
http://www.4004.com/4004-ad.htm
http://thinkofthat.net/2011/04/20/how-to-market-to-real-people-a-lesson-from-apple-circa-1984/
http://9to5google.com/
https://itunes.apple.com/us/app/facebook/id284882215?mt=8
https://twitter.com/twitter
http://www.telco.com/blog/page/3/

Robotics:
Time
http://content.time.com/time/covers/0,16641,19801208,00.html
Rover
apod.nasa.gov
Amazon Drone
http://www.amazon.com/b?node=8037720011
UBER
http://www.nytimes.com/2012/12/03/technology/app-maker-uber-hits-regulatory-snarl.html?pagewanted=all
ASIMO
http://www.wirefresh.com/hondas-asimo-robot-turns-9-shakes-a-leg/
FEMALE ROBOT
http://news.cnet.com/japans-latest-supermodel-a-robot/
Boston Dynamic
http://www.engadget.com/2013/12/14/google-bought-boston-dynamics-its-over-for-humans/
Army general
http://www.digitaltrends.com/cool-tech/u-s-army-interested-in-robots-requiring-little-human-interaction/

Biotechnology:
Watson and Crick DNA Model
http://www.thehistoryblog.com/archives/25193
Humulin
http://www.clinixplus.com/products.php?product=Humulin-R-100-IU%7B47%7Dml-Regular-(-Insulin-Human-Injection-rDNA-Origin-Natural-)-10ml-by-Eli-Lilly-and-Company-%7B47%7D-Injection#.UwtoD_ldW_E
or
http://www.quizbiology.com/2013/04/biology-quiz-on-biotechnology.html#.UwtpaPldW_E
Dolly the Sheep
http://www.roslin.ed.ac.uk/public-interest/dolly-the-sheep/a-life-of-dolly/
Wheelchair
http://illumin.usc.edu/printer/240/thought-controlled-wheelchair/
Zac Vawter
http://www.huffingtonpost.com/2012/10/31/zac-vawter-man-with-bioni_n_2049090.html
Meat
http://www.extremetech.com/extreme/163107-worlds-first-lab-grown-burger-eaten-by-humans-tastes-like-despair
Bionic Eye
http://news.softpedia.com/newsImage/FDA-Approved-Bionic-Eye-Will-Soon-Be-Commercially-Available-in-the-US-389375-2.jpg/

Nanotechnology:
Richard Feynman
http://stupidityandscience.wordpress.com/tag/richard-feynman/
Different photo:
http://www.theguardian.com/science/2011/may/15/quantum-man-richard-feynman-review
IBM 35
http://www-03.ibm.com/press/us/en/photo/28500.wss

Babalot
http://www.tennisindustrymag.com/articles/2004/08/higher_education.html
Invisibility
http://www.telegraph.co.uk/science/science-news/7477954/Harry-Potter-invisibility-cloak-prototype-created-by-scientists.html
Bulletproof Suit
http://www.sunsetvillagepark.com/modules/com_docman/bullet-proof-suit-1765.html
787
http://blog.heartland.org/2013/08/technical-glitches-and-payments-for-down-time-still-nag-boeings-dreamliner/
Lithium Ion
http://insideevs.com/panasonic-to-deliver-100-millionth-lithium-ion-cell-for-tesla-model-s-by-end-of-june/
Abraxane
http://www.abraxane.com.au/
Penn State Badding
http://science.psu.edu/news-and-events/2012-news/Badding12-2012
Stanford Nanotubes
http://news.stanford.edu/news/2013/september/carbon-nanotube-computer-092513.html

ACKNOWLEDGMENTS

Unveiling the trends that pose the greatest threat to long-term corporate operations has been an interesting and exciting challenge. This project has been enjoyable to complete, and we acknowledge with gratitude the entire Global Tectonics team for its members' dedication to this report, from its conception to its conclusion.

Our journey to a final product consisted of several phases. At first, through conversations with top executives and in-depth research, we ensured the key issues originally identified would continue to provide the framework for the future. With these 12 trends pinpointed and an additional one on robotics determined, we then began the difficult task of researching and reporting on each trend. Moving from trend to trend, we made sure each chapter was up to date with the current and future times. When needed, we supplemented and revised the original chapters with additional information that has become integral to the business landscape.

Kathleen Loughran, who served as project coordinator, researched and updated many of the chapters herself, and helped to copyedit the final text. Research assistants Christopher Gerhardt and Nico Zavaleta, both undergraduate students in the Penn State Schreyer Honors College, compiled data and composed graphics for many of the updated charts and graphs. We must also thank Hortense Fong for her help with biotechnology specifically, and Schreyer student Carl Boswell for his research and writing on robotics. Additionally, we appreciate the Center for Global Business Studies' business manager, Nancy Dull, for her help in coordinating multiple aspects and resources needed for the project's completion.

We are also indebted to the Center for Strategic and International Studies and to the members of the advisory board of the Center for Global Business Studies at Penn State's Smeal College of Business, including: Michel Amsalem, Nabeel M. Amudi, James Boland, Jim Clay, George Consolver, William Davidson, Robert Hamilton, Robert Joyce, Marianne Kah, Gerald Kessler, Laura Kohler, Yoon Park, Robert Svensk and

Zhixiang Zhang. As always, they have all been very generous with their time, energy and support. We are also grateful for Smeal College of Business Dean Charles Whiteman, who is steadfast in his support and vision for intellectual excellence.

At the very least, we hope our hard work and research kindles discussions about the future business environment, as corporations prepared for the "earthquakes" we predict will not come crumbling down. We trust this project will stimulate preparation for the inevitable changes we know as Global Tectonics.

ABOUT THE AUTHORS

Fariborz Ghadar is the William A. Schreyer Professor of Global Management, Policies and Planning, the Founding Director of the Center for Global Business Studies at Penn State, and a Senior Advisor and Distinguished Scholar at The Center for Strategic and International Studies. He is a leading authority on future business trends, global economic assessment, the petroleum industry, immigration, international finance and banking, and global corporate strategy and implementation.

As well as be a scholar and author of 15 books and numerous articles, Dr. Ghadar serves as a consultant to a score of major corporations, governments, and government agencies, and he regularly conducts programs for executives of major multinational corporations in the United States and abroad. He also teaches in the executive education programs at Dartmouth, Duke, Carnegie Mellon, and Harvard Business School.

Dr. Ghadar is also the recipient of multiple awards, including three-time Weyerhaeuser Educator of Year Awards, CIO Magazine's Global Leaders Award, and BusinessWeek named him one of the top 10 Stars of Finance. Additionally, Dr. Ghadar is frequently quoted in internationally circulated publications such as the Wall Street Journal, Financial Times, The Washington Post, USA Today, and the Christian Science Monitor.

Erik Peterson is Partner and Managing Director of the Global Business Policy Council at A.T. Kearney. Erik came to A.T. Kearney in 2010 from the Center for Strategic and International Studies, where he was senior vice president and held the CSIS William Schreyer Chair in Global Analysis. Before joining CSIS, he was director of research at Kissinger Associates. He serves on several advisory boards, including the Center for Global Business Studies at the Pennsylvania State University and the Center for the Study of the Presidency and Congress.

ABOUT THE CENTER FOR GLOBAL BUSINESS STUDIES

Global business is growing at over twice the rate of domestic business. Spawned by this growth are international business issues that embody various regions and disciplines. As global business continues to grow and the economies of the world's nations become increasingly interdependent, the management of the firm will require a global perspective. The Center for Global Business Studies at Pennsylvania State University's Smeal College of Business specializes in research concerning emerging functional business issues that shape the global environment. Its mission is to construct a coherent global perspective in business management, research, and education.

Alliances with corporations and institutions around the world offer many opportunities, as well as challenges. Businesses and universities working together to educate executives and students can share their knowledge of the most recent business practices, theories, and research. Communication among this broad and international group requires long-distance educational opportunities offered through the use of new technologies. The Center for Global Business Studies is poised to link corporations and Penn State together and to deliver programs for this diverse audience. Additionally, the Center for Global Business Studies' research efforts are geared — and relevant — to industry. Working closely with an advisory board made up of a cross-section of distinguished global business leaders, the Center for Global Business Studies advises and directs various research projects.

Made in the USA
Lexington, KY
18 August 2014